The Message Glorious

His Promises Are Good Enough For You

By Barbara Radmacher
As Told By Doris Kemp

Psalm 115:1
Barb Radmacher

Copyright © 2020 by Barbara Radmacher.

ISBN	Softcover	978-1-951886-62-2
	Ebook	978-1-951886-63-9

All rights reserved. No part of this book may be reproduced or transmitted in any form or by any means, electronic or mechanical, including photocopying, recording, or by any information storage and retrieval system without express written permission from the author, except in the case of brief quotations embodied in critical reviews and certain other non-commercial uses permitted by copyright law.

The Scripture versions cited in this book are identified in Appendix 2, which hereby becomes a part of this copyright page.

Printed in the United States of America.

Book Vine Press
2516 Highland Dr.
Palatine, IL 60067

Give of thy sons to bear the message glorious;
Give of thy wealth to speed them on their way;
Pour out thy soul for them in prayer victorious;
And all thou spendeth Jesus will repay.

from the gospel hymn "O Zion Haste"
by Mary A. Thomson (1834-1923)

* * *

My reasons for writing this book:

- That God will be glorified
- That others will be helped
- That our family and friends will always remember the story of our brave son, David, and our miracle Down's son, Scott. (What a 'glorious message' both are from the Father above!)

* * *

Build a little fence of trust around today;
Fill the space with loving deeds, and therein stay.
Look not through the sheltering bars upon tomorrow;
God will help you bear what comes of joy and sorrow.

Mary F. Butts (1836-1902)

I want this book to not be a recounting of the sad/bad things that have happened to us as a family, but a book of praise for God's faithfulness in the midst of these happenings. The Lord has been our anchor for these many years, and the 'message glorious' that I want to convey to all who read these pages is – 'God's promises are good enough for you!'

* * *

Know therefore that the Lord God, He is God, the faithful God which keepeth covenant and mercy with them that love Him and keep His commandments to a thousand generations.

Deuteronomy 7:9 KJV

DEDICATION

Only be careful and watch yourselves closely so that you do not forget the things your eyes have seen or let them slip from your heart as long as you live. Teach them to your children and to their children after them.

Deuteronomy 4:9 NIV

This book is being written in order that our descendants; the children, the grandchildren, the great-grandchildren will know about our journey through the last half of the 20th Century and the beginning of the 21st (*hard as it is for me to believe it is here!*). My prayer is that they will see God's faithfulness in all situations and realize how He sustained us through all circumstances.

To my children: Jerry, Barbara, Peggy Ann (*in Heaven*), David (*in Heaven*), Frank, and Scott

To my grandchildren: Melodee, Tony, Gregg, Michael, Jason, Reed, Shannon, and Kelley.

To my great-grandchildren: Kathleen Anne, Madison Leslie, Duncan Jerry, Avery Jordan, Carlin Joy, Lydia Grace, Logan Scott, Ava Grace, Oliver Tate, Alex Nathaniel and Andrew Lee.

To those precious additions: Judy, Bill, Lisa, Duncan, Vicki, Kimberly, Laura, Joe, Derrick, Rita and Dana.

To my soul mate, Lloyd, now with our Heavenly Father.

And to Jesus Christ, the Lord of my life, who continues daily to renew our strength and guide us with His strong right hand.

INTRODUCTION

Without faith it is impossible to please God.

Hebrews 11:6a NIV

Have you ever met someone who, like a pack rat, saves everything? Well, meet one now! I've always saved, especially anything with words. Words have always fascinated me. I've saved quotes, notes, poems and stories that struck my fancy. I've saved lists and receipts, thoughts and happenings.

You see, I've always had what I call a 'willy-nilly' mind, one that runs in two or three directions at once. So, in order to have some semblance of keeping my thoughts and memories straight, I've written many of them down.

For many years now, I've kept a combination prayer journal/diary. Why? I could be praying very sincerely to the Lord and my mind would wander off. Maybe I would wonder what I was going to have for supper, or some such. I read somewhere that if you would write out your prayers; your thoughts would not wander. That has proven true for me.

Another bad habit I had was telling people I would pray for them and later, upon seeing them, they would thank me for praying. I would think, 'did I?' or 'didn't I?'. For years now, I have made notes to myself for prayer requests, and I stick them in my purse and then record them later in my journal. If I write your request in my journal, I can guarantee you I pray over that request. An added bonus is going back through the journals and seeing the awesome ways God has answered those prayers (*often in ways I would never have fathomed!*).

The following quotes I had written in a little black notebook I kept years before many of the happenings in this book. I'm sure the Lord had me copy them to be used, in later years, for encouragement and comfort.

> **"The response that pleases God most is our confidence in Him in spite of circumstances that we do not fully understand."**
>
> **anon**

> **"We cannot always give thanks for the circumstances we are in, but we can give thanks to God for His love and care in the circumstances. He may not have ordered the circumstances, but He is in them to work out even the most grievous situation for our good."**
>
> **anon**

I've often felt the Lord nudging me to write my story. Over and over messages came through to me, and I knew I should be testifying to God's faithfulness as it has been proven again and again in my life.

My grandson, Jason, is a confident, passionate minister in New York City…*yet I can still see him as a 12 year-old absolutely petrified with fear of thunderstorms, begging me, "Pray! Oh pray, Gram!" and then shouting, "Well, it's not working!"* From one of Jason's sermons I read, 'If those who know the story of God's faithfulness do not tell it then how will it be told?'

Joel 1:3 says 'Tell it to your children and let their children tell it to their children, and their children to the next generation.'

NIV

If for no other reason, here then is my story.

SEEING GOD'S PLAN

"In Him (Christ) we were also chosen, having been predestined according to the plan of Him who works out everything in conformity with the purpose of His will."

Ephesians 1:11 NIV

Despite my blessed childhood, I grew up as a very insecure and mixed-up girl. As I look back, I am amazed at the way God led and directed my life choices even when I frivolously lived my days ignoring His presence. God had a plan!

MY SHAKY BEGINNINGS

Chapter 1

For it is God who works in you to will and to act according to His good purpose.

Philippians 2:13 NIV

Way down in Southern Indiana about twenty miles from the Ohio River and the Kentucky shore, nestled among the rolling hills, is the small town of Corydon. Now, lest you think this is an insignificant little hamlet, I want you to know our Corydon is steeped in history. It was once the Territorial Capital of the Indiana Territory and, later, the first state capital of Indiana. The Old State Capitol building has been preserved and also the Court Yard which I dearly love.

It was in this little town that God placed me, and I've lived all of my 85 years either in the town or within four or five miles of it.

* * *

I want you to know I was a very timid, insecure, mixed-up little girl. School was always very difficult for me because of my overwhelming self-consciousness. Where that came from, I do not know. My parents were loving and supportive, yet I floundered in my own self-doubts. I did love to read and would often, as a child, escape my insecure world into books.

In my teen years, boys and popularity became my obsessions and, amidst my constant pity-parties, I strove to become popular by any means. I was on completely the wrong track!

Well, in the midst of all those mixed-up years, I made one wise, right choice and I know now, even though I didn't know then, the Lord had a hand in it. That was my choice of a husband. It surely was a marriage smiled on in Heaven for it lasted from January 19, 1941, until the Lord took him Home on February 22, 2000.

"Two are better than one, because together they can work more effectively. If one of them falls down, the other can help him up..."

Ecclesiastes 4:9 TEV

When we married, Lloyd had a good job at the Keller Manufacturing Company (*a factory started in the 1800's by my grandfather and two of his brothers and a brother-in-law*). At the time of our marriage, Lloyd's salary was $12 a week. (*Wow! But, you know, we did very well.*) We gave Mom and Dad $5 a week to live with them, and we had $7 a week to blow. We went to the local movie (*called the 'picture show' then*) every time the movie changed. We had no car so we, pretty well, walked everywhere we went.

Lloyd was 6-feet 4-inches and 225 pounds....very handsome in the eyes of his adoring, but insecure little wife. What a wonderful, faithful husband and father he was! His family were church going, saintly people, praying people. Lloyd was saved when he was twelve years old, although when I met and married him, he had backslidden. (*Of course he had or he wouldn't have picked me as a life-long partner!*)

My two loves, even as a child, were babies and books. The birth of our first child in 1942 was the beginning of my 'growing up.' I quit being just an insecure wife and became an insecure mother as well.

For the first time in my life I felt responsibility. (*I've always said my children have taught me so much.*) Our daughter, Barbara Elaine, joined Jerry Lynn in 1946. We were so pleased to have both a boy and a girl.

In 1949, our doctor sent me to bed in the fourth month of my third pregnancy. Things just did not go well in this pregnancy. I stayed in bed 2 ½ months. A girl was hired to care for the children and me.

It was a very stressful time, and the more stressed I got, the more I smoked. (*In those days, it was considered a sin for a woman to smoke, but there was never anything said about the dangers to your health or to your baby's well being.*) I hid my smoking from my dear in-laws whom I loved so much and who were so good to me.

I remember during the long months of bed rest, I took the Bible Lloyd had brought into our marriage and placed it on the back of the couch; the couch where I spent most of my time. For some reason I just felt better with it there. Occasionally I would take it down, open it and try to read it, but the words didn't speak to me in any way. I wondered, "What do people see in this that gives them hope and encouragement?" I know now that, without the Holy Spirit within me, the words were just words with no understanding and no power.

> ***Jesus said, "But the Counselor, the Holy Spirit, whom the Father will send in my name, will teach you all things and will remind you of everything I have said to you."***
>
> ***John 14:26 NIV***

At 6 ½ months, another precious little girl was born in our home. She looked perfect, even to fingernails and toenails, black curly hair, weighing about 1 ½ - 2 pounds, about the size of one of Barbara's smallest dolls.

The Red Cross brought an incubator into our home for our Peggy Ann. Her Daddy sat right by her, watching her through the night; but after 15 hours our little one was taken back to Heaven. What a precious little dear she was. She left an empty place in my heart that is still there.

I was unable to go to her funeral, but the minister came to see me after the funeral. He told me that the Lord had seen that the baby was just too weak to make it down here, and He had stooped down and took her up into His arms. Well, that was food for thought to me. I now had a little one in Heaven. I doubted I would go there, considering my life choices; but that kind of thinking I would push out of my mind without much thought about right or wrong or changing my ways.

I'm sure now that, even then, the Lord was chipping away at the hardness of my heart.

* * *

I had joined the church Lloyd and his family attended. I joined for one reason only and that was so my husband and I could belong to the same church. In fact, that's how the minister of the church approached me about joining. I met him on the street in Corydon one day and he said, "Doris, don't you want to join the church Easter Sunday? We're taking in several people and, you know, Lloyd is a member and then you'd both belong to the same church." I said I would and I did. I answered 'yes' to all the questions and became a member in name only. It made no impact on the way I was living day to day....one big pity-party...smoking, drinking, carrying one big heartache over the loss of the baby, and striving to be a good mother and wife. (*How mixed up can one person get?*)

* * *

A little over 57 years ago, we moved into our present home. This is the first and only home Lloyd and I ever owned. We were both so glad to have a home of our own. It was four rooms, no running water, in fact – no water at all. Lloyd and Jerry dug a cistern in the back yard and concreted it. We had water hauled to fill it, and we drew water out of the cistern, a bucket at a time, for any water needs we had – drinking, washing clothes and dishes, cooking, and bathing. Our only toilet was at the end of the back yard.

(*One evening, some years later, as I was pouring water I had boiled on the wood stove into the large washtub we placed in the kitchen for baths, one of the boys commented that he wished we had a real bathtub like he had seen at my brother's house. When I told my sister-in-law what he had said, she laughed and said her son had wished they had a bathroom outside in the yard like we did!*)

Lloyd was so happy with the new place. He had always wanted to farm and have animals. We now had 8 ½ acres. Lloyd enjoyed working in the soil. He also cut wood for our wood stoves. He worked as an auto mechanic by day and, usually, continued working long into the evenings keeping the home fires burning (*literally and figuratively!*). Our lives, of course, revolved around the children.

David Earl was born in January of '52, another premature baby at 4 pounds; but he was born in our new local hospital and, with the good care he received, he survived and we took him home when he weighed 5 pounds.

I was a very busy mother, and I spent a lot of time feeling sorry for myself. I had many fears and hang-ups. My worldly ways were beginning to concern me. The life I was living without Jesus was becoming very, very uncomfortable.

FROM DARKNESS INTO THE LIGHT

Chapter 2

> ***....that you may declare the praises of Him who called you out of the darkness and into His wonderful light.***
>
> ***1 Peter 2:9b NIV***

I had been a habitual smoker of cigarettes from the time I was fourteen. One day, I came face to face with the reality of my situation when I walked into the living room and there was my darling daughter, Barbara, playing with her dolls with a piece of paper rolled up, pretending to smoke.

I grabbed it out of her mouth and (*of all things*) shouted, "Barbara, nice little girls don't do that!" (*How absurd!*) Wide-eyed, she looked up at me and said, "But Mommy....you do." From then on, I knew I had to quit smoking.

It was a long, hard struggle for many months; and I finally realized I didn't have the ability to quit, weak willed as I was. As I was cooking supper one evening, I had just thrown my last cigarette into the old woodstove; and I wanted a cigarette so bad I could have crawled in after it. I leaned against the counter and cried out (*the first sincere prayer I had ever spoken!*), "O dear Lord, I want to quit so bad. Could you please help me?" Well, this is the gospel truth. The craving for cigarettes left me, and I've never smoked another cigarette since that day!

This episode left me even more mixed up in thoughts and feelings. The amazing thing to me in looking back is that, even though this turmoil raged inside of me, no one else seemed to notice. Just me and the Lord knew about it.

About this time, I had started listening to radio preachers. One morning, a preacher talked about 'the Good Shepherd.' He used as an illustration the painting by Bernard Plockhorst, *a very familiar print.* He said, "Notice Jesus carrying the baby lamb. Most people think that little lamb was so weak he couldn't make it, so Jesus picked it up and carried it right next to His heart." (*That is exactly what our minister had told me about Peggy Ann!*)

But this radio minister went on, "Now that could have been the case, but notice in the picture the Mother Ewe is walking right by the side of Jesus, looking up at Him and the baby lamb." He said that old mother ewe probably wouldn't stay close to the flock, and she would run away and do bad things; so Jesus reached down and picked up her lamb, that she loved very dearly, and when He did, the mother ewe never strayed from His side again. * * * * * * I realized later that this was another way the Lord was speaking to me.

(*All through the years, I could not remember the name of this radio preacher who was instrumental in setting me on the path to my salvation. I felt I was probably listening to the Back to the Bible Broadcast. In January 2001, when I was reading a book by Erwin Lutzer, this story was mentioned and he quoted James Vernon McGee, the Back to the Bible radio preacher.*)

God always has a purpose --- a purpose and a plan.

When David was nearly two years old, I walked down the aisle of our United Brethren Church, knelt at the altar and invited Jesus to be my Savior and Lord of my life. My life has been changed ever since. I became a person of joy in the Lord instead of a 'pity-party person.' The Lord has been my strength and my fortress since that happy day.

'Happy day, happy day,
When Jesus washed my sins away,
He taught me how to watch and pray
And live rejoicing every day,
Happy day, O happy day.'

by Phillip Doddridge (1702-1752)

Lloyd also came back to the Christian way, but he was never as vocal about his walk as I have been. It was the difference in our personalities I think, but I truly believe we complimented each other.

I was very vocal about Jesus and, in my newfound faith, maybe a little too zealous. I was out to save the world! My dear husband was very down to earth, full of common sense and, at the same time, of a strong faith, just much less vocal about it.

(*I recall one day Lloyd and I were working together in the garden; and I was on my newfound Christian soapbox preaching away when Lloyd stopped, turned toward me, and said, "Doris, if I wasn't already a Christian, you would really turn me off!"*)

Anyway, I think we worked pretty well together in establishing a Christian home. There have been many joys and many sorrows, many ups and many downs, but through it all, the Lord has remained faithful.

In 1955, the Lord gave us another son, a healthy 8½ pound boy, Frank (*Lewis Franklin only on his birth certificate*). (*Do you not think it was good that I did not have the ill effects of smoking and alcohol in my system at this time? I think Frank's birth weight reflects that!*)

Our little house was bursting at the seams, but I hold dear to my heart all the joys we had as a family within those walls. In late summer of 1957, I wrote this prayer that God has answered in so many ways.

> **My prayer to God is that He would take these children (Jerry, Barbara, David and Frank), His gifts to me, and these little ones He is using to help me grow and mature as a Christian, and that He would use them all of their lives to glorify Him and spread the message glorious.** (*This was my first recorded reference to the title of my book.*)

Home and church were our mainstays, plus the love and caring from our extended family. We spent each Sunday with Lloyd's mother (*Grandma Kemp*) and his sister (*Auntie*). My folks also lived close by, and we shared many happy times together. Also, they were always there for us in the trials and sadnesses that came along.

In January of the next year, my only sister was killed in an automobile accident, leaving six children, the youngest the same age as our Frank, two. My mother and I cared for the four younger children for several months (*the two teenagers stayed in Louisville with their father*). Mother worked in an office, so Lloyd and I had the children in our home most of the time.

Can you picture eight children and two adults in a four-room house without many of the conveniences of today – i.e. bathroom, running water, washer and dryer? In looking back, I wonder: how did we manage? – what did I cook? – where did we sleep? Well, as I often tell my grandchildren, we just 'made do with what we had,' *something they know little about nowadays.*

I'm so glad I was no longer a PPP (*pity-party-person*). I remember that winter I quilted three quilts. I always said I quilted them with stitches and tears. Through those months, I learned that God always makes a way. He is faithful!

My brother-in-law married again in the summer of that same year. He married a wonderful woman whom we all grew to love. She was a wonderful homemaker and mother for those children.

A STRAWBERRY MIRACLE

Chapter 3

"Hear my prayer, O Lord, listen to my plea! Answer me because you are faithful and righteous."

Psalm 143:1 NLT

In the late 50's, Lloyd was working as a mechanic (*now called an automobile technician!*). With our family of four children, we were struggling financially; striving to make ends meet, letting one bill go to pay another, and more in debt all the time.

One evening while reading my Bible, I came across a question in the last book of the Old Testament that popped right out at me. "Will a man rob God?" Immediately, in my heart I said, "Lord, you know that I would never rob you." Then, I went ahead reading.... "You have robbed me of the offering and tithes due me." (Malachi 3:8). Now, at the time, we attended church every Sunday and gave in the offering plate, but not nearly a tithe.

So I approached Lloyd and read him the Scriptures. He said, "I know, Doris, and if you show me how we can pay our bills and get out of debt, then we will tithe our income." Well, I could think of no way to do that, so we went on as we were, but it continued to bother me.

Spring came and our strawberries were looking good. Now, the strawberry patch was my project. I loved picking strawberries. I told Lloyd that if I had any berries to sell, I wanted to tithe the money and he said okay.

It started raining and raining and the weeds in my big berry patch grew and grew. Now, those of you who have ever raised berries know that, in order to have an abundant crop, you have to give those plants room to grow and keep the patch free of weeds. There was no way I could win 'the battle of the weeds' that year.

Well, the strawberries finally started to ripen and God really did a miracle. No one could believe the beautiful berries that came out of that weedy berry patch. I picked and picked from morning to evening. Lloyd's mother came and took care of the house and children, and I picked and picked.

A neighbor up the road bought all the berries as I picked them and took the produce into the city to sell. I took a tenth of all the money I earned and put it in an old pitcher that we kept in the top of our glass-doored cupboard; and on Sundays we gave the money for the Lord's work.

I wish I had kept a record so I could tell you how much it amounted to, but I didn't. Believe me when I say, it was a definite miracle. Never again did the strawberries flourish as they did that year.

From that time on, every bit of money that has come into our household has had the tithe from it placed in the old pitcher and given to the Lord.

Now, I could say that, from then on we have been rich and full-handed, but those of you that know us would know I was making that up. But it wasn't long after that when we were making our bills and were debt free – another miracle. Through the years, God has been faithful; and our needs, maybe not all of our wants, but our needs, have been met.

Every child and grandchild in our family knows this story, and knows of the old pitcher that held God's money until we took it into the storehouse.

God is faithful......We serve an awesome God.

QUIET TIMES

Chapter 4

Being confident of this, that He who began a good work in you will carry it on to completion until the day of Christ Jesus.

Philippians 1:6 NIV

In the beginning of the 60's, things were going pretty smoothly in our little corner of the world. We were your normal mid-western family. Money was tight, but our needs were met. We were in church every time the doors were opened. The children were healthy. David had always been prone to colds and ear infections, but even those seemed to have disappeared as he was getting older.

David and Frank were inseparable buddies. Barbara was a teenager, and Jerry had graduated from college (*working himself through*) and was teaching his first year. He and his wife, Judy, had presented us with our first grandchild, Melodee Lynn.

The Lord continued to bless my faith walk. Finding time to spend with the Lord, reading His Word and praying, was not easy with our bustling family to tend to. My dear sisters in Christ at our church often helped me to stay on track. Together we signed commitment cards saying we would spend fifteen minutes a day communicating with God. I remember sitting at our kitchen table, early in the morning, with the alarm clock set before me. I thought, 'what will I talk about for 15 minutes?' (*That astounds me now, for I often spend an hour with the Lord and it seems like only minutes!*)

Once again, my love of reading came to my aid. So many great Christian writers offered me advice and encouragement: Catherine Marshall, Norman Vincent Peale, Corrie Ten Boom, Hannah Whiteall Smith, and Dale Evans Rogers to name a few. I followed their advice as to ways to spend quality time with God and learn to 'listen' for His responses to me.

* * *

(*Now at 85 years of age, my quiet times are not only a time to communicate with my dear Savior, but also a time to recuperate, physically and mentally, as well. I call them my 'blessing breaks'.*)

DAVID'S STORY

As the spirit of the Lord works within us, we become more and more like Him, and reflect His glory even more.

2 Corinthians 3:18 NLT (paraphrased)

He was a normal little boy, our son David; fighting with his brother, embarrassing his teenage sister by clowning on the school bus while rolling his eyes up into his head so only the 'whites' were visible. He would say he had finished his homework, then half an hour before bus time, remember something he had forgotten and cause mass confusion in our tiny home in the minutes before the bus arrived. Yes, he had many of the typical little boy defects.

But, in the last two years of his life, he lived a lifetime; lived it victoriously. I feel he fulfilled his mission, and spread the message glorious in his beautiful, simple, little-boy way. The Holy Spirit surely did dwell in the heart of our little Davey.

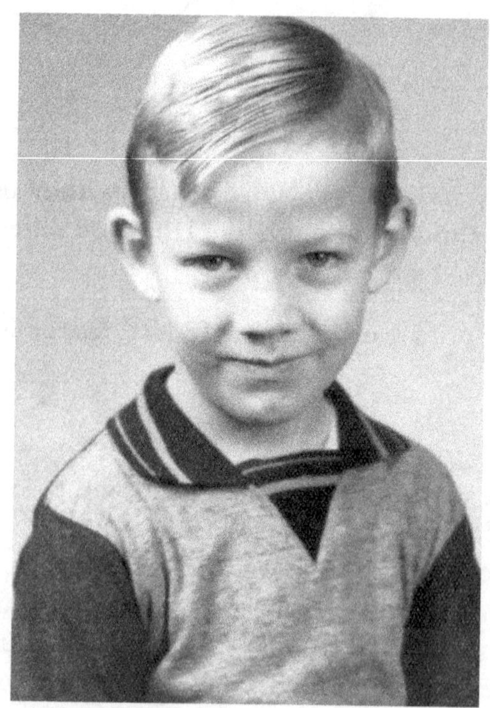

David Earl Kemp

CANCER STRIKES

Chapter 5

"Fear not, for I am with you. Do not be dismayed. I am your God. I will strengthen you; I will help you; I will uphold you with my victorious right hand."

Isaiah 41:10 NKJV

It was 1963, ten days before school would be out for the summer; a day like any other in our little corner of the world. Lloyd and I had started our garden. I was thinking about spring- cleaning as I picked up sticks in the yard so we could mow. It was about time for the school bus to arrive, and I knew things would liven up when David and Frank, 11 and 8, and Barbara, a teenager, bounded off. Occasionally, I had to play the role of peacemaker when the kids arrived home, but more often, instead of managing disputes, I simply had to keep up with my very active children.

David and Frank were inseparable buddies. While they had their usual brotherly disagreements, they were normally engrossed in happy, playing times: running, jumping, playing ball, fishing, and climbing trees.

On this day, however, when the bus doors opened, they did not release my scampering, boisterous children. Instead, David gingerly stepped off, followed by his brother and sister. He limped over to me, complaining that his knee hurt. I told David he probably hurt it playing ball at school, and that the pain would go away over night.

The next morning, however, David awoke with a high fever and complained that the pain in his knee was worse than ever. So, off to the doctor we went. Our dear family doctor thought it best to put David in the local hospital for tests and x-rays. The tests indicated David had rheumatic fever. Rest was recommended.

Thus began a difficult summer of resting and doctoring. David, always so active, was confined to the house for most of what was supposed to be a carefree summer recess. And the pain, always in his knee, was excruciating at times.

As the lazy days of summer headed toward fall, it was obvious David was not getting any better. In September, we took him to see a specialist in Louisville, at what was then called Children's Hospital. The doctor who examined Davey found a knot on his side behind his pelvic bone. He thought it was cancer.

Exploratory surgery was scheduled immediately. Half way through the surgery, a doctor came out to give us a report. I had walked out into the hallway to get a drink of water, and was standing there alone when the doctor walked up to me.

"Mrs. Kemp," he began, "I am sorry but..." and that was as far as he got. I came as near fainting as I have ever come in my life. I thought David had died on the operating table. The doctor grabbed me to keep me from falling. "Oh, Mrs. Kemp," he exclaimed, "He's all right, but we couldn't get out all of the tumor. He made it through the surgery all right."

The surgeons had discovered a large tumor on David's pelvic bone and removed what they could. They said it was the kind of cancer that would spread and that it would be terminal. (*Sometimes doctors can be so blunt!*)

A time of treatments followed: good days and bad days. We held onto the Lord, and I read over and over my 'refrigerator promise.'

> **Build a little fence of trust around today;**
> **Fill the space with loving deeds, and therein stay;**
> **Look not through the sheltering bars upon tomorrow;**
> **God will help thee bear what comes of joy and sorrow.**
>
> **Mary F. Butts (1836-1902)**

Davey's love for everyone around him and his little-boy love for life were an inspiration to all of us. We were all bound together in love and the God whom we loved sustained us.

THE LITTLE SPARROW

Chapter 6

> ***Not even a sparrow…can fall to the ground without your Father knowing it. So don't be afraid* (David)*; you are more valuable to Him than a whole flock of sparrows.***
>
> ***Matthew 10:29&31 NLT***

Lloyd and I had given the boys a BB gun for Christmas the year before David became ill. (*I'm sure Lloyd looked forward to the days – I mean the nights – when the boys would accompany him on coon hunts.*)- Frank rigged up a target in the back yard that Davey could shoot at while sitting on the steps of the porch. Davey was shooting from there one day late that summer. Suddenly, he flung open the screen door and burst into the kitchen, holding a little dead bird in his hands.

With tears streaming down his cheeks, he cried, "Look what I did, Mom! I killed this little bird! I killed it! I killed it!"

"Well, honey," I said, "Why did you aim at it?"

"Oh, I didn't think I could hit it," he cried, "but I did, I did!"

I tried to console him by telling him the little bird was insignificant; that sparrows were pests, building their nests where they shouldn't and eating the chicken feed. But Davey would not be consoled and grieved, for some time, over that little bird.

Not helping the matter, Davey discovered in his Bible that Jesus said sparrows were precious to the Father and not one fell to the ground without His knowing it. I could only remind Davey that Jesus goes on to say we are of greater value to our Heavenly Father than many sparrows.

Needless to say, Davey never aimed his gun at anything with life in it again.

* * *

December of 1963 arrived and Christmas was fast approaching. So was the arrival of our 6th child. (*Yes, I was pregnant when David was diagnosed. During the first months of my pregnancy, I had thought, at the age of 41, I was probably going through the mid-life change.)* For the first time in my childbearing years, I paid little attention to myself and my pregnancy; my focus was so much on Davey.

On December 6th, I wrote Psalm 138:3 in my Upper Room devotional: "***In the day when I cried thou answerest me, and strengthenest me with strength in my soul. KJV*** How I clung to that Scripture as the day of my delivery approached!

On December 10th, God sent us a very special gift; an eight and a half pound boy, a boy we named Scott Douglas. I breezed through the delivery and was only in the hospital two days. I was motivated by the desire to get back home to my family and, especially, to David. I am certain the Lord was, indeed, strengthening me as I had cried out to Him.

The day after Scott was born, David talked Barbara into taking him to the Fair Store so he could buy a card for me. Making decisions was always hard for David, and Barbara vowed and declared he read and debated over every card in the store that day. She was really losing patience with him, when he finally stated he had found the perfect card. Barbara told him the card wasn't even an appropriate card for the birth of a baby, but David said, "It's just right for Mom!"

Wouldn't you know the card was about a sparrow and a robin? It's a lovely card. I still have it, and I cherish it. It certainly was the perfect card for me.

By Elizabeth Cheney - 1858

May He who cares
for alll of us
Be with you, day by day,
To bless and cheer
and strengthen you
In His own loving way.

Love always
David

(Oh David, I know now why you couldn't be consoled about the little dead sparrow. O Father, help us all to love and appreciate life, even life in a tiny little sparrow, just as Davey did!)

If God sees the sparrow fall
Paints the lilies short and tall
Gives the skies their azure blue
Will He not then care for you?

anon

ONE DAY AT A TIME

Chapter 7

And the peace of God, which transcends all understanding will guard your hearts and your minds in Christ Jesus.

Philippians 4:7 NIV

That Christmas was a very special time. Davey was doing better, and the new baby, so good and healthy, was a precious gift to the family. I remember sitting in the rocking chair with Scott on Christmas Eve and feeling such a wonderful sense of peace. That night our entire immediate family was all gathered under our roof. I thought, 'We are all here together and safe. Thank you, Jesus!'

* * *

1964 – a year chock full. Yes, days of suffering and anguish, but miracles of God's sustaining love and grace....our beautiful, smiling baby .... family and friends love and support....Davey's love of life, and his deep, abiding faith in God.

In February of that year, we took Davey to the hospital for a check-up, and it was discovered that the cancer was spreading rapidly. Intensive treatments were recommended.

David's hair falling out was a big concern to Lloyd and me as he began these stronger sessions of cobalt. I decided to talk to Davey about this, fearing he would be devastated when it happened. His reply was, "Oh well, Mom, I'll just get a wig like Randy Atcher's." Now T-Bar-V Ranch on television was a favorite show for David and Frank. They always laughed, saying Randy never had his wig on straight. (*The wonderful thing was that, though David's hair thinned some, he never lost it all. Many times our 'what if's' are bigger than what really happens!*)

* * *

Pain control was not nearly as effective at that time as it is now days, and Davey suffered much too much. I lost count of the many times we were in Children's Hospital and our own local hospital.

That year time 'stood still' for us, and we all learned to live one day at a time. I had always been a person that looked forward to some future time; when I would be 16, instead of 14, when the babies would be older, and on and on. During that time, however, I too learned to look for the blessings in each day and thank God for them.

Our family and friends gathered around to support us. Lloyd always came home for lunch, a comfort to the family if the day was stretching long. He did all the grocery shopping. When David needed to be taken to the hospital in Louisville for treatments, Lloyd's boss always arranged for him to be off work. My dear mother took time off from her job to make the trip with them so I could stay with the baby.

Our dear Aunt Mayme and Uncle Ted made frequent thirty-mile trips to visit. If Davey was having a bad day and they drove up he would say, "Well, here comes Aunt Mayme. She'll know what to do."

I could probably count on one hand the number of times Davey, the baby, and I attended a church service during the last year of Davey's illness. But when we couldn't go to church, the people brought the church to us. By that I mean they were Christ's hands, feet and Spirit to serve us. These dear ones prayed with us, carried in food, sat with us, and took our other children to school and church functions. They were the visible signs to us of 'Christ's love.'

> ***"Be full of love for others, following the example of Christ..."***
>
> ***Ephesians 5:2a LB***

* * *

I recall others who were like ships passing in the night...those angels God sent our way to make our journey a little bit easier. There were special nurses who joked and tended to Davey in his many hospital visits. One sweet nurse always sat with me while I ate in the hospital cafeteria, offering me solace and a shoulder to cry on.

During one of David's first hospital stays, he was placed in a room with Jack, a distinguished businessman from Chicago. Jack had a serious heart condition. He and his wife traveled to Louisville to get the best heart surgeon available. Jack and Davey became fast friends. Lloyd, David, and I prayed with Jack and his wife prior to Jack's surgery, and we followed his recovery after he was released from the hospital.

Jack sent Davey a baseball autographed by Pee Wee Reese (a Louisville native), Sandy Kofax, and other members of the Los Angeles Dodgers of the early '60s. Davey was so proud of that baseball, often showing it to his visitors and telling them about Jack.

The next summer my mother received a letter from Jack's wife telling of his death. We never did tell Davey, but when Davey died in October, I often thought of him and Jack sharing good times in Heaven.

Davey received hundreds of cards and liked to look at and read them over and over. The question of the day became, "Well, how many did the mailman bring today?" One dear lady from our church, then in her 90's, fixed a card for Davey with dimes taped to it, and a Scripture verse by each dime for Davey to open each day of the week. How he enjoyed that card, and so many others thoughtful people sent.

The cards and prayers of the people also brought comfort and strength to the rest of us. I saved every card and read and re-read them.

Here's a verse from one of them:

"I join with you in a little prayer
Because- well just because I care
Like a bird in a storm-swept land
I see you safe in God's right hand
No power can part you from His care
Keep faith for God is everywhere."

anon

(*Never doubt the great benefit your cards and prayers can be to other folk. The dear Lord knows I try to be faithful in prayer, but I'm afraid I'm a big failure when it comes to sending cards!*)

A lady from the church gave David a parakeet, cage and all. How excited we were for we had heard how much enjoyment they were when they talked. David named him 'Tweety', and he soon became a part of our family. We bought a book, "How to Teach Your Parakeet to Talk"; and David spent hours and hours coaxing Tweety to speak. Finally, we resigned ourselves to the fact that our Tweety was only going to tweet. He wasn't going to talk, and he never did.

(*About four years after Davey passed away....on a cold winter night, we were all sitting around eating popcorn. Tweety flew down off his perch, I gave him a grain of popcorn, and off he flew back to his perch. He ate the popcorn and immediately fell over dead. I know! I know! Popcorn is not birdseed! But Tweety had always enjoyed popcorn and I felt it was just his time!*)

* * *

So many people were attentive and faithful to Davey during his illness.

One of these was my dear Aunt Mabel. She worked in Louisville at Stewart's, a very plush store. She was a very dignified and classy lady, but she showered love and attention on our Davey. She sent cards almost daily, brought him gifts, and took him for rides in her fancy new car. He carried her picture with him all the time, and called her his 'beautiful aunt.' She surely was a wonderful encourager to him.

Years later, as Aunt Mabel reached her 90's, it fell upon my daughter, Barbara, and me to care for her. At times, the task would become very trying, but we would spur each other on by thinking our Davey was probably looking down on us and saying, "There's my mom and sister, caring for my 'beautiful aunt'....94 and still beautiful....how happy it makes me that she still loves life, still sends cards of encouragement....and how she loves You, O Father!"

A tribute to Aunt Mabel written by Barbara

A Grand Dame, (whom my Dad affectionately referred to as Miss Daisy). She loved people, and was recognized and loved at Granny's Cafeteria by people from Corydon, to Louisville, to England. She dressed impeccably and coordinated every outfit. No one I have ever known could better choose matching accessories and just the right jewelry to set off an outfit perfectly.

She loved life, and people, and the Lord. She had strong opinions and voiced them often. Many a letter or phone call to congressmen came from Ms. Mabel Pinne. She was a very selective shopper, and found ways to make her desires known to those who served her.

She was unique.
She was loved.

* * *

On top of my desk there is a miniature lamp filled with perfume (*my last Christmas gift from David*), and a picture of Davey holding in his hands his Charlie Weaver joke book. He is smiling from ear to ear. How he loved to read the jokes aloud to me and anyone else who would listen. We knew the jokes almost 'by rote'; he read them so often. I told people that was when I learned to laugh on the outside while crying on the inside.

We wanted to make each day special for Davey because we knew our days with him were limited. That's when we learned to live 'one day at a time'.

Turn loose of yesterday for it is gone.
Do not reach for tomorrow for it has not come.
Grab today for it is here.

—anon

David

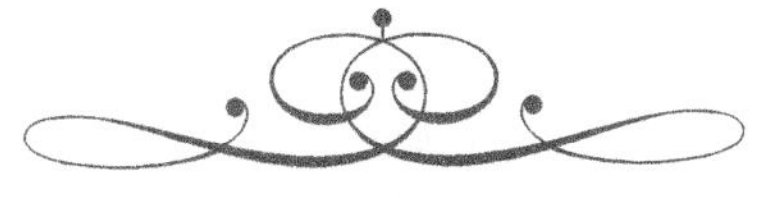

AREN'T HIS PROMISES GOOD ENOUGH?

Chapter 8

The Lord is faithful to all His promises and loving toward all He has made.

Psalm 145:13b NIV

One evening David was lying on the couch resting, having just returned from another round of cobalt treatments. While doing the evening supper chores, I took an occasional glance at him to assure myself that he was all right. Davey looked so helpless and I felt that in some way I must reassure him of Jesus' love and be very sure he had a personal relationship with Jesus.

Now we had a Christian home. Davey, along with the rest of the family, attended almost every worship service our church offered. When Frank was born Lloyd had taken David, who was three at the time, to an eight-night revival at our church. Lloyd sang in the choir, and David sat by himself on the front pew. Many from our congregation commented on David's rapt attention to the service and how he always kept his eyes on his Dad.

However, he was just a little boy and I felt that I had to be sure he had received the Truths he had been taught. So I went into the living room and knelt beside him. In my stumbling way, I told him that if he ever had any questions about life, or death, or God; he could always tell me and I would be ready to listen.

"What do you mean, Mom?" he asked.

"Well Davey," I began, "When I was a little girl about your age, I would hear people talking about 'being saved' and 'not being saved.' It always scared me a little and I would wonder, 'was I?' or 'wasn't I?'. Even now Davey, even after being a Christian for ten years, with so much happening, I have some doubts about some things." (*I was really fumbling for words!*)

Suddenly Davey looked me straight in the eye, took my hand in his and said, "What's the matter, Mom, aren't His promises good enough for you?"

Wow! *How many times over the years have I been reminded of Davey's strong and simple faith and his searing query.... "What's the matter, Mom, aren't His promises good enough for you?"*

* * *

Standing on the promises that cannot fail,
When the howling storms of doubt and fear assail;
By the living word of God, I shall prevail,
Standing on the promises of God.

Standing, standing,
standing on the promises of God, my Savior.
Standing, standing,
I'm standing on the promises of God.

One of my favorite hymns
by R. Kelso Carter (1849-1926)

LITTLE BOY ON THE SUNPORCH

Chapter 9

'And the Lord, He it is that doth go before thee; He will be with thee, He will not fail thee, neither forsake thee; fear not, neither be dismayed.'

Deuteronomy 31:8 KJV

Our local hospital in 1964 was becoming too small for the patient load, so the beautiful sun porch had been divided into two rooms for patients. These rooms were totally glassed in and surrounded by beautiful trees. Davey always said that if he had to be in the hospital, he wanted to be in one of the sunrooms. The nurses and doctor usually managed to get him in one of them.

In 1981, seventeen years after Davey's death, I was on a phone calling committee, making calls to elderly shut-ins. I phoned Mrs. Deaton who had worked for years as a nurse's aide at the hospital. When I told her my name, she said, "Oh, you're the mother of the little boy on the sun porch!" (*Oh Davey, what an impact you had on people. What a blessed privilege to be known as the mother of the little boy on the sun porch.*)

* * *

Mother Kemp had a cross-stitched sampler on her living room wall that said:

'To know how sweet your home may be,
just go away – but keep the key.'

Every time we would go there, David would read the sampler using his own version.

'To know how sweet your home may be,
just go to the hospital!'

No matter that it didn't rhyme. It was exactly right.

* * *

All the times Davey was in the hospital, he was never left alone. I stayed during the daytime and his Dad stayed every night, after working all day. Lloyd's mother and sister and my mother and dad offered second homes to our other children. God gave us all extra strength, patience, and endurance.

One morning in the hospital, I asked David if I could sit for a spell on the bench outside his room while the cleaning lady was straightening up. David said, "Yes, if I can just see you."

I sat on the bench and recalled how Frank, when only four or five years old, would often peer in the back screen door while playing outside, just to make sure I was there. Later, I found the notation I had made in my journal about that.

My little boy knows full well that I would never leave him alone. When he is playing outside, if he is hurt, frightened or needs anything he runs to me. But there are other times when he just comes to the back door and peers in. One glimpse of me and he goes back to play. He just needs to be reassured of my presence.

How like my little boys are we, the children of God? We know He is always with us, this He has promised, but we need those times of reassurance.

For God has said, 'Never will I leave you,
Never will I forsake you.'

Hebrews 13:5 NIV

* * *

One morning, when we were spending a few of our many days away from home and in the hospital, I had walked down to the hospital lounge while Davey was being bathed. I was sitting alone, praying and crying. My Christian friend, Ann, happened to walk by with her little boy, and seeing me, she immediately rushed to my side and asked if she could pray with me. She knelt on her knees in that crowded, public room and prayed aloud to our Lord asking Him to give us His comfort and His mercy. How I was touched and strengthened by her witness!

On another day when Davey was feeling better, I said to him, "Davey, you could walk up and down the hall and stop at each room and spread a little sunshine." "Yes, Mom," he responded, "I could tell those who don't know Him about Jesus." But then he proceeded to say he would have one problem, and he folded his hands, looked up at me and said, "You know, don't you Mom?" And I did know.... the weakness he felt in being able to witness and pray with people he didn't know. I thought this was understandable in a little twelve-year old boy, but how many of us have reached maturity and would still have this problem.

(*O Lord, give us a 'Holy Boldness' in praying with others whenever and wherever the opportunity arises. Amen.*)

PRECIOUS MEMORIES

Chapter 10

"But watch out! Be careful never to forget what you yourself have seen. Do not let these memories escape from your mind as long as you live! And be sure to pass them on to your children and grandchildren."

Deuteronomy 4:9 NLT

In May of 1964, our daughter Barbara graduated from high school. Davey, Scott, and I could not attend and Jerry, our oldest son, and Judy, a special daughter-in-law, brought Melodee, our precious first granddaughter, to stay with us while they all attended the graduation ceremony. Melodee, at thirteen months, missed her mommy and daddy terribly, and the only way she would be consoled was for Davey to sing "On the Good Ship Lollipop" to her. He sang it over and over and over again. Never do I hear that old Shirley Temple tune that I do not think of that time.

How precious all situations were, and the memories are still vivid and comforting!

* * *

Davey had a keen sense of humor and always enjoyed a good joke. I think he would have pulled some terrific practical jokes as an adult.

A friend dropped by one summer afternoon with some bright red cherry tomatoes. We didn't grow this type tomato, and Davey said they sure did look like cherries. Then he said, "I'm gonna fool Frank when he comes in!" When Frank came running in, David immediately went to work. "Look Frank! We got some great lookin' cherries. Have one!" Frank plopped one in his mouth as David howled with glee, knowing Frank never liked tomatoes!

* * *

David always wanted to have something to do with his hands. We had several catch-all drawers that the whole family threw 'odd-and-ends' into. David loved to go through those drawers. He called it 'cleaning out clutter.'

* * *

One afternoon, Davey was in excruciating pain, and we were trying to think of something to do to get his mind off it. "Bring me my paints," he said, "and a piece of white cloth."

This is what he made.

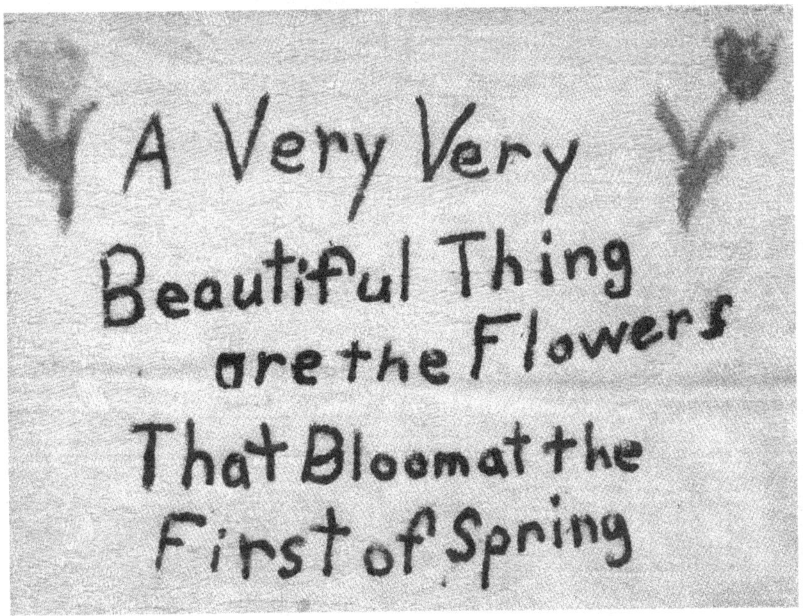

By the time he finished his painting, the pain medicine had taken effect and life was bearable again. I have the painting framed and on our mantel to remind me to keep my thoughts on the beautiful things God has created.

* * *

One evening, I was in the kitchen preparing supper and I heard singing coming from the bedroom. I stepped to the door and there was our brave little one sitting up in bed singing…

"When upon life's billows you are tempest tossed,
When you are discouraged thinking all is lost,
Count your many blessings, name them one by one
And it will surprise you what the Lord has done…"

by Johnson Oatman, Jr. (1897-1922)

On and on he sang. He never knew I was standing there listening, but I got the message. Many times when life gets weary, I sing and try to count my blessings just as David did so many years ago.

* * *

We had good times when we lived life to the hilt, and then there were the days when our dear boy's suffering was so intense… medicine, massaging, praying, and trying to think of beautiful things….nothing could take away the pain.

On just such a day, we (*his Dad and I*) were kneeling by his bed, doing all we knew to do, when suddenly his Dad put his arms around him and cried out, "Oh, David, if I could I would climb in that bed and hurt for you!"

Finally the pain subsided and David went to sleep. Later I mulled over this incident. I thought, that's what true love is……

loving someone so much that we would take their place in suffering if we could. Then I thought of God's love for us.

'For God so loved the world, that He gave His only begotten Son, that whosoever believeth in Him, shall not perish but have everlasting life.'

John 3:16 KJV

My prayer:

> **'O Lord, Fill us with your love that we might spread it here on earth. Amen.'**

* * *

Fishing in our farm pond had always been one of Davey's favorite passions. He spent many an hour cleaning his tackle box, even after he was bedfast. I would spread a newspaper on his bed, and he would spend hours shining his fishing flies and sorting his corks and all the rest of the fishing treasures you fishermen have in your tackle boxes. He often said that he sure hoped there was a fishing spot in Heaven for him. (*Yes, he did realize the seriousness of his illness.*)

Shortly after Davey's death, an evangelist was holding a revival in our church and I asked him that very question. He answered, "Oh yes, my dear! The Bible says a river runs through the New Jerusalem." *I believe it is well stocked with fish!*

* * *

On the fourth of July in '64, we celebrated as we always have, by having a cookout and fireworks in our back yard. Davey watched from the back porch in his wheelchair. As usual, we had a great family time.

The next morning was Sunday and, while everyone except Davey, the baby, and I were in church, Davey developed a terrible headache. It only got worse and worse. I called our doctor, and he said to bring him to the hospital. Then I called the church, and our pastor came with Lloyd and we took Davey to the hospital.

It turned out to be a cerebral hemorrhage, and Davey fell into a coma. They told us he might pull through but they didn't think he would ever be himself again. He might recognize us, but that would be about all. They placed him in an oxygen tent, and Lloyd and I sat for hours with our hands under the tent holding his hand.

God gave us a miracle. Day by day, Davey grew more responsive and alert.

One day, while I was holding his hand he said, "Well Mom, you can turn loose of my hand now. I have somebody else's hand to hold on to." Thinking he was hallucinating I said, "Who do you mean, Davey?" "Well Mom, you know," he said and pointed upward. I am convinced God had sent one of His Heavenly Messengers (the Scriptures call them 'angels') to hold his hand and encourage him.

'For the angel of the Lord guards all who fear Him (those who revere and worship Him) and He rescues them.'

Psalm 34:7 ASV

* * *

David soon decided that the next thing he would do was to go to the County Fair in late August. To encourage him everyone who visited, and even some of the wonderful nurses, kept giving him money to spend at the Fair. I'm sure they all thought he would never go…but, guess what? Another miracle happened and, one afternoon in late August, Davey got to go to the Fair. He was in a wheelchair and our dear son, Jerry, pushed him around the rough gravel roads at the fairgrounds.

Davey had a wonderful time. He talked about his good time at the fair for days and days.

One fall afternoon, Aunt Rea and my mother stopped in for a visit. They wanted me to go for a ride with them, thinking I needed to get away for a little bit. I wouldn't go. I can still feel those bony little arms hugging me tightly after they left. "Thanks for being such a good Mom." Davey said.

There are so many special Mom moments that I will always treasure.

David loved to have me read this Scripture to him. I would read it over and over and put in his name.

(From Jesus)
Peace I leave with you (David),
My peace I give unto you (David),
Not as the world giveth
Give I unto you (David).
Let not your heart be troubled (David);
Neither let it be afraid.

John 14:27 KJV

David loved sunsets and the maple tree in front of our house. In the fall, its branches stood proudly, filled with beautifully colored leaves....and all our precious memories. David always called it 'my beautiful tree.' (*I'll tell you the story of David's maple tree later in this book.*)

THE AUTUMN OF DAVID'S LIFE

Chapter 11

"For now we see through a glass, darkly;
But then face to face: Now I know in part;
But then I shall know even as also I am known.
And now abideth faith, hope and love, these three;
But the greatest of these is love."

1 Corinthians 13:12&13 KJV

Autumn – my very favorite time of year! The beauty of the red, yellow, and golden leaves - apple-butter makin' time, -school days. I have fond memories of kicking the leaves as I walked to school as a child. The smell of burning leaves brings back deep feelings of nostalgia. As a lover of words, even the word 'autumn' is, to me, one of the most beautiful words in the English language.

One of those beautiful autumn days will stand out in my memory until the Lord takes me home. I know that day God gave me a definite message, not in an audible voice, but in one of those up close and personal moments that you know, that you know, that it is God speaking.

I believe this day was the beginning of this book.

* * *

October in our little town in Southern Indiana is a beautiful, wonderful time. We are nestled in a valley surrounded by rolling hills, and by mid-October the trees are in full color – beautiful reds, oranges, yellows and greens.

I was standing and looking out the hospital window early one October morning, gazing out over our sleepy town tucked down under the hill on which the hospital stands. On this particular morning, God had caused the sun to shine on the autumn leaves with an awesome brightness. I thought to myself, "A God who can make a world so beautiful can surely take David's illness and year and a half of suffering and make something beautiful out of it."

I prayed, "O Lord, you have made the world so beautiful. The Scripture says you 'make everything beautiful in its own time' (*Ecclesiastes 3:11*). God, don't let David's two years of fighting this awful disease be in vain, for naught. You are all powerful. You can take this time and work it for good. Make something beautiful out of it God."

It was as if God was telling me, "Doris, there is a glorious message in all of this! There is a purpose in everything and, although you can't see it now, later on you will."

* * *

Those last weeks were ones of increased suffering for David and I'm so thankful to hear that pain management is much improved nowadays.

Our pastor spent much time with us and one day when David's pain was overwhelming him, Rev. Chamberlin said, "David, try to think of something beautiful." David responded, "I've done that a million times."

Our little boy was getting tired.

* * *

One day we were trying to talk Davey into taking a shot for his pain. He hated shots with a passion and continued to refuse to take it, despite our best coaxing. My mother came to visit on her lunch hour and in her matter of fact, no-nonsense manner said, "Now, David, the shot will help your pain and you just must take it!" David said, "No, I won't!" and the two of them began to verbally spar. He finally relented and took the shot, but the tension between the two of them hung over the room.

Finally, my mother said, "Well, I need to get back to work now" and started to pick up her purse. "Wait, Grandma! Come over here!" David shouted and, as she drew close, he flung his thin arms around her neck and said, "Oh Grandma! I just love you in spite of everything!"

I'm so thankful my mother received this assurance of David's love and forgiveness. He taught us all a valuable lesson that day.

> ***"Therefore if you have any encouragement from being united with Christ, if any comfort from His love, if any common sharing with the Spirit, if any tenderness or compassion, then make my joy complete by being like-minded, having the same love, being one in the Spirit and of one mind.***
>
> ***Philippians 2:1&2 TNIV***

* * *

Three days before David's death the pain was so severe. He had been given medication, but it failed to dull the terrible pain. In desperation, I said, "Well, David, there just isn't anything else we can do!" Looking up at me, he said, "Yes, there is Mom. We can pray. You pray first and then I will." I don't remember my exact words, but I'm sure I asked for the pain to leave. I will never forget his clear little boy voice as he prayed.

"Dear Lord, If there is anything under mankind...anything that you can do to help the doctors and nurses to make me well... would you please! Please! Amen.

That night the pain left. Davey went into a coma and he didn't hurt anymore.

Although there was nothing under mankind that could be done at that time, great strides have been made in treating cancers since that day. In every lonely laboratory where men and women work feverishly in cancer research, God is answering David's prayer. Researchers are diligently working, sorting out the reasons cells become cancerous and developing therapies to stop cells from growing into tumors. Someday – maybe even this day – there will be cures for little boys and girls and men and women with this terrible disease.

Thirty-two years later, my grandson Michael and I were sitting in the swing in the front yard under David's beautiful maple tree. Michael was home from college. I read the above notes from my journal to him. "Oh Gram!" he said, "that is what I'm going to be doing…trying to find a cure for cancer!" He has now finished graduate school at North Carolina State University, has worked at the National Cancer Institute and is now doing research at Ohio State University.

God's faithfulness is awesome!!

> ***"Tell it to your children and let their children tell it to their children, and their children to the next generation."***
>
> ***Joel 1:3 NIV***

David endeared himself so to the nurses and doctors who cared for him.

One of the nurses came into the room after just arriving on duty and saw that, during the night, David had gone into a coma. She cried and said she couldn't sleep the night before because she was thinking about him and how he was suffering. She said she had prayed fervently that God would relieve his suffering and she now felt this coma was an answer to that prayer. We all felt that way.

The morning David passed away, the head nurse came in and stood at the foot of Davey's bed with her hands behind her back. (*I later found out that she had a hypodermic needle to calm Lloyd and me, if need be, when David drew his last breath.*)

Our minister was there, and I'd never felt the presence of the Lord like that before. Lloyd and I stood with our arms around each other as our precious son quietly quit breathing. He had gone home. His suffering was over.

As we walked quietly down the hall, I heard sobbing coming from one of the rooms. As I stopped and peered in, I saw it was one of the faithful nurse's aides who had helped care for Davey and she was sobbing uncontrollably. I walked into the room and put my arms around her and comforted her, telling her to remember how Davey loved Jesus, and I was sure he went straight to be with Him.

Afterwards, I thought it was sort of ironic, me comforting her, but, you see, I had just experienced God's presence in such a mighty way. Later, when the loneliness settled in, I too had to be comforted.

When Rev. Chamberlin preached Davey's funeral, he told about the mighty presence of God in Davey's hospital room the day that Davey went home.

The presence of our Lord carried us through those days immediately following David's death. We could only feel a calm, sweet peace that our young soldier had gone home and wasn't hurting anymore. God surely was very, very close.

"God is faithful
His love endures forever."

from Psalm 138

We chose this poem to be used on the commemorative leaflet given to visitors at the funeral home. Our daughter, Barbara, tells me she read it over and over during David's funeral service to keep from sobbing.

God has not promised skies always blue,
Flower strewn pathways all our lives through;
God has not promised sun without rain,
Joy without sorrow, peace without pain.

But God has promised strength for the day,
Rest for the labor, light for the way,
Grace for the trials, help from above,
Unfailing sympathy, undying love.

by Annie J. Flint (1866-1932)

* * *

As we stood at Davey's casket for the last time, Lloyd put his arm around me and said, "Remember what Davey said." I knew he was referring to God's promises. We both knew only God could carry us through.

Someone gave me a copy of the hymn 'He Giveth More Grace' and it became a special blessing to me. I placed it on our refrigerator and read it often. I think the author and I are 'kindred spirits.'

He giveth more grace as our burdens grow greater,
He sendeth more strength as our labors increase;
To added afflictions He addeth His mercy,
To multiplied trials, He multiplies peace.

When we have exhausted our store of endurance,
When our strength has failed ere the day is half done,
When we reach the end of our hoarded resources
Our Father's full giving is only begun.

His love has no limits, His grace has no measure,
His power no boundary known unto men;
For out of His infinite riches in Jesus
He giveth and giveth and giveth again.
Annie J. Flint (1866-1932)

* * *

Davey died at the end of October and the winter loomed big ahead of us. I had God's promises in Scripture that I read and hung onto each day. We felt God's presence with us at all times; and yet, the loss was so keen, and many times grief would overwhelm us.

Lloyd's sister and her husband came from California and stayed all winter. I've told everyone that we could not have made it without all the people God sent our way to help us: Mother Kemp, Clella, the church family and friends, my own dear parents and our devoted children.

Many times we would sit down to a meal....(*I don't know why when you've given up a loved one, meal times bring it all back – always an empty place I guess*); but there was Scott between Lloyd and me in his high chair, laughing, and cooing, and doing the happy things babies do. We would soon lose our sadness by concentrating on him and his antics.

God is so good – He is merciful and full of love.

A few weeks after we buried David, and during one of our frequent visits to the cemetery, I made a promise to my Davey and to myself and God that I would not spend my time grieving but would live and love every precious moment of life just as Davey had done.

> ***1 Thessalonians 4:13 & 14 says;***
> ***"But I would not have you be ignorant...concerning them which are asleep, that ye sorrow not even as others which have no hope. For if we believe that Jesus died and rose again, even so them also which sleep in Jesus will God bring with Him." KJV***

In the days and months following David's death, I found myself drawn to that Scripture again and again. I fervently believed (*and believe!*) that death is not the end of our story. When Christ returns, we will all be reunited, never to suffer and die again. I did not want to grieve as one who had no hope. I would tell myself, "This could happen today, and I don't want to be sorrowing like someone without hope when the Lord returns to take us all home together."

Day by day by day, with God's and our friends and family support, we made it through.

I copied this poem in my little black notebook during the winter after Davey passed away.

> **When we go home, I hope to see**
> **a sweet, young face look straight at me**
> **unchanged from what it used to be**
> **When we go home.**

When we go home, t'will be to hear
a darling voice, so low and clear
our hearts are thrilled to think it near
When we go home.
When we go home – it must be so
our Savior's wondrous face to see
and praise Him through eternity
When we go home.

anon

I don't know what Heaven will be like, but I hope to see my sweet, sweet David restored to perfect health; and be able to cradle my precious Peggy Ann in my arms once more.

* * *

Several months after Davey died, during a period when the loneliness, for me, was almost unbearable, Phyllis Cunningham sang the song "We'll Talk it Over in the Bye and Bye" (by Ira F. Stanphill – 1949) during a church service. What a solace and comfort it was to me. I had written her a note telling her how much it meant to me and, years later at a Sunday evening service, she told about the note I'd sent her and she sang this song again 'just for me.' What a precious song, and what a dear sister in Christ.

* * *

Yes! God's promises have proven good enough for me!

My Lord says:

"I will turn their mourning into gladness.
I will give them comfort and joy instead of sorrow."

Jeremiah 31:13 NIV

Oh yes, grief and longing for my little Davey at times overtook me; my mourning was keen. I'm so thankful, though, that I know the rest of the story, and my Savior promises that one sweet day.... **"There will be no more death or mourning or crying or pain, for the old order of things has passed away." Revelation 21:4 NIV**

DAVID'S LEGACY

Chapter 12

We will not hide them from their children;
We will tell the next generation the praiseworthy deeds of the Lord, His power, and the wonders He has done.

Psalm 78:4 NIV

What an impact David had on the people who knew him and, also, the ones who never met him, but have been told about him and his witness to what the Lord does for us even in the midst of the worst of times. All the grandchildren and great-grandchildren who have joined our family since 1964 have been told over and over our Davey stories, of his deep faith, and the many 'gems of truth' he left with us.

* * *

Our daughter, Barbara, who has been a nurse for over 35 years, has always said David had a mission here on earth and truly fulfilled it in his twelve short years. I had always felt David's illness and suffering had had an influence on Barbara's choosing the nursing profession, but it wasn't until a few years ago she shared with me the exact time that she made that decision.

She said that I had left her in the hospital room with David, and he started hurting real bad and begged her to do something to help him. It was not time for more medicine, but she said the nurse came in and started comforting David and rearranging his pillows. She decided then that she was going to go to nursing school and learn what to do to help hurting people…and she spent all of these years doing just that.

* * *

David's closest friend Mike's eyes filled with tears even years later when we talked about David. While David was bedfast, Mike would come on his bike; come in and just sit by David's bedside.

Sometimes they would talk – sometimes Mike would just sit there. What a beautiful friend!

* * *

In 1999, my granddaughter Shannon wrote an essay about David for her college English class. Here is an excerpt: 'Many people would think a child this young would blame God for this terrible disease and turn their backs on Him. This was not the case for David. He stood strong in his beliefs.'

And she closed with this: 'It is hoped that all the people who hear this story will be touched. The pain this poor boy went through may help the world someday because the people who were touched by him may come through on their promises to help others with this excruciating disease.'

* * *

My grandson, Michael, while working on his doctorate at North Carolina State, wrote this to me in a letter: 'I feel that Davey's life had a direct impact on the course my life has taken. I always considered it quite an honor that I was named after David, at least my middle name. Many times I lose my focus. I start to get frustrated with the length of my schooling and worry about finding a job once I do graduate. Writing this, however, has helped me remember what got me interested in all this and has reassured me that this is the path God has set before me. Love, Michael.'

* * *

You see, God used this terrible tragedy in our life. He brought 'good' out of the 'bad.' He used David's life and testimony to give us lessons we will never, ever forget. We must carry on his legacy and witness to the next generation....and the next....and the next.

* * *

God continues to assure me of His hold on my life. I claim Isaiah 46:3 & 4 as my promise from God.

> ***'Listen to me, all Israel who are left*** *(Doris).* ***I have created and cared for you since you were born. I will be your God all thru your lifetime, yes even when your hair is white with age*** *(mine is now gray!).* ***I made you and I will care for you. I will carry you along and be your Savior.'***
>
> ***Isaiah 46:3 4 NLT (paraphrased)***

THANK YOU, JESUS!

SCOTT'S STORY

For you created my inmost being;
You knit me together in my mother's womb.
I praise you because I am fearfully and wonderfully made;
Your works are wonderful,
I know that full well.

Psalm 139:13&14 NIV

I think the Lord sent our son, Scott, as a special blessing to our family. He has touched so many lives and blessed us all with his special, unconditional brand of love.

Our pastor during Scott's teen years recently wrote him a note saying, "Scott, you have been a real blessing to me and I am truly grateful for the years I was your pastor in Corydon. You taught me patience and a new way to express love and a very simple way to say thank you to the Lord. Thank you, Friend!"

Scott Douglas Kemp

DOWN'S DIAGNOSIS

Chapter 13

"You saw me before I was born. Every day of my life was recorded in Your book. Every moment was laid out before a single day had passed."

Psalm 139:16 NLT

When Davey died, Scott was ten months old. He had just started sitting up. He didn't crawl or attempt to walk. I had recognized, in the months before, that Scott was slower to reach those 'baby milestones' we mothers expect. One day in the hospital before Davey passed, I had asked our dear family doctor if he didn't think Scott was slower than other children his age. The doctor put his arm around my shoulder and said, "Oh, Doris, it's been so long since you had a baby, you've just forgotten. All children are different."

Now, I'm sure the doctor knew from the day of Scott's birth that he was a Down's baby. (*The attending nurse at Scott's delivery, who became a close friend of mine, told me years later that they both knew and decided it would be best not to tell us at that time.*) I'm also convinced God had His hand in that situation. We had accepted Scott just as the blessing he was (*and is!*), and we had placed no limits on his abilities.

We felt so blessed by Scott's presence, and he was such a happy, healthy baby. We doted on him and praised his every accomplishment.

I became, for him, the schoolteacher I had always wanted to be in my youth. I learned, early on, that Scott had his own slow, steady pace. (*This slow, steady pace has continued into his adulthood and, I confess, frustrates me more now than it ever did in his childhood!*) Praise! Praise! Praise! Encourage! Encourage! Encourage! Push! Push! Push! became my bywords. (*But don't all children respond well to those same words? Praise! Encourage! Push!*).

* * *

Shortly after Davey's death, my daughter had encouraged me to volunteer at our local hospital. The time I spent there was definitely a healing time for me.

One day, while volunteering in the gift shop, another lady and I were talking about our children. I told her how I worked with Scott and had to encourage and encourage him. She said, "I don't know how you do it! My son got an 'F' on a test at school, and I stayed awake all night worrying about it!" "Oh," I said, "I just can't let myself worry about what he can't do, but must just praise him for what he can do!"

* * *

Early on, I recognized Scott's great love for music. As a baby, he was often quieted by music. Porter Wagoner had a half-hour program on TV in the evenings, about the time I would start to fix supper for the family. I would place Scott in his playpen, and he would be perfectly content just to listen, hardly moving, just taking it all in. I used to say Porter Wagoner was my baby-sitter while I prepared the meals.

When Scott was a little older, we bought him a little piano with the play-by-color notes. The grandsons always enjoyed playing on it too, but from the next room, I could always tell when Scott was playing because his love and keen ear for music came out even then. I suppose then was planted in my heart a drive to help him do something with this talent God had given him.

Scott also loved to be read to, and I love books, so I read to him constantly. It was easy to recognize that he understood what I was reading to him and this pleased me greatly. When Barbara would come home from college, she also would read to him, even reading Shakespeare's plays and sonnets aloud. (*When we mention this now, Scott says, "Oh Orick, I knew thee well!" --not a Scott memory, I think, but just a normal Scott response.*)

* * *

Scott wrote this poem. I love the 'Oh! To!' instead of 'Ode to.'

Ob!te a Friend

A Friend That is Always There
A FriEn/ that is Always Near
+ Friend That is Always true
Thats Why I Love you

We quickly discovered that Scott required different 'tactics' than we had used on the other children to redirect his behavior. One evening when Scott was about four years old, Lloyd was working in the barn, and Scott was digging in the dirt outside the barn. I went to tell Scott it was time to come in to get ready for bed. Scott said, "No!" and would not get up off the ground.

Lloyd came out of the barn and in his deep, commanding voice said, "Now, Scott, go with your mother into the house." "No!" Scott replied. Lloyd was not used to being defied and said, "No son of mine tells me 'no' like that! Now get up and go into the house with your mother!" "No!" Scott defiantly exclaimed.

Lloyd spanked him and said, "Go into the house!" "No!" ......

Lloyd spanked him again. Scott cried, but remained resolute....

"No!" Lloyd turned to me and said, "Doris, I just don't know what to do with him. You'll have to handle him!"

I said, "Scott, let's play a game. It's called the train game. Do you want to be the engine or the caboose?" Scott stood up, chose 'caboose,' and we went into the house to get ready for bed. When Scott started school, we played the train game nearly every morning to get him up and ready for the school bus on time.

SCHOOL DAYS

Chapter 14

"For I know the plans I have for you," declares the Lord. "Plans to prosper you and not to harm you, plans to give you hope and a future."

Jeremiah 29:11 NIV

When Scott was five years old, we took him to enroll in kindergarten. The lady who was registering the children took one look at Scott and stated, in a very blunt way, "I'm sorry, Mrs. Kemp, but we just can't accept a Down's Syndrome child." Now, this took me by surprise for, though I knew he was slow, I had never heard the term 'Down's Syndrome.' I took my precious Scott's hand and walked back to the car where Lloyd sat waiting for us. I said to Lloyd, "They wouldn't take him and said we would have to find a special school." How I was buoyed up by my dear husband's response – "Well, Hon, at least we get to keep *him*!"

* * *

At the time, the only school in our county accepting Down's Syndrome children was fifteen miles away in Palmyra. The plan was for Scott to ride our regular school bus to the high school, and then transfer to the 'Crusade Van' that would take him to Palmyra.

The first morning Frank, thirteen at the time, carried a kicking and screaming Scott to the bus. I spent the morning pacing the floor, crying, and praying. I kept saying aloud, "This is for his own good! This is for his own good!" I might not have believed it at the time, but I said it!

Scott started half-day kindergarten, and Lloyd would go to pick him up at noon. The staff soon reported to us that Scott would spend most of the morning watching out the window for his Dad's truck. They suggested that Scott spend the full day and come home on the bus. Once we developed that schedule, Scott settled in well and truly enjoyed school.

At first, they concentrated on teaching Scott self-care; dressing, brushing his teeth, manners, and so forth. I began to wonder if this would be the extent of his education, just learning to tend to himself. But then, they began to work on counting (*always a challenge for Scott*) and phonics (*which to Scott became the key to learning to read*).

The teachers and aides were so loving and attentive to Scott, and he responded so well to their leading. I'm sure they faced some frustrations dealing with Scott's little idiosyncrasies. For example, he could not resist a light switch and loved to turn lights off and on and off and on. He was always on the move, actually hyperactive then (*which those who know him now cannot fathom!*).

Words have always fascinated Scott and, to this day, he often makes good puns using words. The teachers told me he loved the word 'thermostat' and would say it over and over again. How I admire their abilities to redirect this tendency Scott has toward repetitive behavior. School was *truly* for his own good!

* * *

Transportation
A Scott story

One day Barbara, Scott, and I went to a Frisch's Restaurant. Barbara stopped off in the bathroom, so Scott and I sat down on the black benches to wait for her. A bejeweled, made-up lady came out of the bathroom and both Scott and I started to get up, thinking it was Barbara. As we sat back down, realizing our mistake, Scott said, "Now, that's what I call a transportation!" (*meaning 'transformation', of course*).

* * *

Scott has always been so happy and loving toward others (*a God-given trait I have found in all Down's children*). His Down's features attracted attention to him, of course; and early on, I decided that if he was happy, I was going to be happy too. Others responded to his love in kind. I remember, one day, asking Scott if the children on the school bus ever laughed at him and he said, "No, they laugh with me!" So be it, I thought.

(In 2004, my grandson, Michael, and his wife asked their four-year old son, Avery, if he had ever noticed that Scott was different. He said, "Yes, I have. He is different." "How is he different, Avery?" Michael asked. "He doesn't have any hair on his head like you have, Daddy," was Avery's reply. Michael said, "Yes, God made us all different." Avery responded, "I can see all the parts of his forehead."

Beautiful! Beautiful! I say. Just like his playmates Gregg, Michael, and Jason never commented on Scott's being different when they were young. The only time it was even eluded to was from kind-hearted, compassionate Gregg who, if I would get cross with Scott, would say, "Now, Gram, you know how Scott is!"

* * *

During Scott's early schooling, they suggested that we take him for evaluation by a professional (*I always called them an expert*). That day the expert took Scott into a room by himself and, after a spell, she called me in. She said, "Well, Mrs. Kemp, Scott has some real problems with learning. You can send him to school if you want to, but I doubt he can really ever learn anything." She went on, "He can't count, he doesn't understand or follow simple instructions', and proceeded to relate all that he couldn't do. I said, "But I read to him all the time and he under-stands!" She looked at me in a pitying way, and said, "Well, honey, you can read to him if you want to, but I doubt he under-stands what you read." I distinctly remember my response. I pounded my fists on the table and said, "Well, he does!" I'm sure I came across to her as a defensive mother.

I've often wondered what kind of show Scott had given her. I feel certain he went into 'shut-down mode' that only escalated with her negative responses.

In years since, with every great accomplishment Scott has made, I've wished this 'expert' could see it. I didn't feel ill toward her, because I'm sure Scott did not give her any hopeful signs that day, but the incident does highlight the importance of not limiting what others are capable of doing.

* * *

In 1970, when Scott was seven, an event happened that I feel had a great impact on Scott's development. Our daughter Barbara's family moved from Evansville to Corydon. Scott and his nephews, Gregg and Michael, became fast buddies. Barbara started working part-time as a nurse, and I babysat for the boys.

Gregg and Michael, and Jason (*who was born in 1975*), readily accepted Scott as their equal and placed no limits on his abilities. They included him in all their play and expected him to join in. If they had to make new rules for a game to keep Scott involved, they all played by those rules.

Joker! Joker! Joker!
A Scott story by Barb

The boys were playing a game of Joker! Joker! Joker! Scott's question: What do you call a place that is hot, has miles and miles of sand, and no water?

Scott – "H-E-L-L?"

Barbara said she had some secret concerns regarding Scott playing safely with her boys, fearing Scott would not fully understand and, unwittingly, hurt one of them. Shortly after their move; however, Gregg was swinging an old golf club and struck Scott in the head with it, requiring a trip to the doctor for stitches. (*Luckily, that one incident was the only time we had to seek medical care for one of the boys while they were in our care…a real miracle, I think!*)

I SURE LOVE THAT JESUS

Chapter 15

"I praise you, Father, Lord of Heaven and earth, because you have hidden these things from the wise and learned, and revealed them to little children."

Matthew 11:25 NIV

Our pastor during Scott's early years, Rev. Nelson Chamberlin, played a major role in Scott's Christian growth. When Scott was ten years old, he was really moved one Sunday morning by the sermon Rev. Chamberlin gave. I'll let Rev. Chamberlin tell that story.

This article appeared in the Old Capitol United Methodist Church Chatter in 1974.

Your Pastor says…

Chalk it up! This past month has to be one of the most exciting, most rewarding months during my entire ministry. Oh yes, there were the obvious things…

There was the fine spirit of acceptance on the part of the congregation of the work the building committee has done over several months. The congregational vote was most encouraging.

There was the excitement of the groundbreaking service on Palm Sunday when the reality of our building project took on real, tangible evidence. People have been saying for 10 years, "I'll believe it when I see it," and now, the doubters have to be convinced.

There was Easter Sunday, a high point in the Christian year, when the people of God assemble in larger numbers than on any other given Sunday.

There were the usual kind people who encourage the minister with comments such as, "I really enjoyed that message this morning" - "Something you said today really got to me" – "That sermon was really helpful."

But the best thing – absolutely THE best thing – that happened this month was a comment a ten-year old boy made

to your minister as he left the worship service on Easter Sunday morning! The little fellow's name is Scotty Kemp. You all know the youngest son of Lloyd and Doris Kemp. Scotty may never grow up to be the world's greatest philosopher or theologian. Learning and understanding sometimes come hard for him. But as the Scripture says, "Out of the mouths of babes…"

As Scotty Kemp left the worship service on Easter Sunday, he put out his pudgy little hand and said to me, "Preacher, I sure do love that Jesus!"

I have thought about that on numerous occasions since. I haven't been able to shake the impact of that statement.

Oh yes, it is nice to hear people compliment you on a job well done. It is exciting to hear words of congratulations on great new beginnings. It is encouraging to know that you are reaching people and helping them. But the thing I will treasure the most is the comment of a little ten-year-old boy who said to me, "Preacher, I sure love that Jesus!"

For, you see, when all is said and done, that is what I'm trying to get people to do…..to "love that Jesus." And whatever else I do as a minister, and whatever we do as a church, if we fail to get people to 'love that Jesus' we have accomplished little of lasting note.

That Jesus I have come to know is the kind of person who is truly worthy of your love. I want you to be able to say you love Him too.

(*I've always thought that day was the beginning of Scott's closer walk with his Savior.*)

Rev. Chamberlin and his wife, LaDonna, returned to Old Capitol in November, 2005 as part of our church's 100th anniversary celebration. An article written by Randy West appeared in our Corydon Democrat, this now some thirty years later. Randy wrote: Before Nelson closed his talk here and the church shared communion, he asked a very special person, Scott Kemp, to come up to the altar area with him. Nelson said Scott is "one of the great heroes in my life" *and then related the "I sure love that Jesus" story.*

* * *

It amazes me the way God has used Scott's life to impact others he meets.

In 1995, our family friend, Randy West, offered to accompany Scott on a spiritual retreat called the Emmaus Walk. How I anguished over sending Scott! Oh, I wanted him to have the experience, but 'what about all his daily routines and habits that might make him stand out as a retarded individual?' The Lord led me, however, to accept this as His will for Scott, and we made plans for Scott to go.

My prayer journal notes, during this time, reveal my deepest thoughts and concerns.

Wednesday, September 27 – O Father, be very near my Scott as we prepare him for the Walk. O Jesus, put your arms of love around this child of yours and help him to be a blessing and inspiration to all around him. Bless Randy, Lord, and, if he has any fears or anxieties, calm him. You know my concerns and anxieties Jesus. I ask that you give me more courage and faith. Teach me to trust You. Amen.

* * *

Thursday, September 28 – This is the day, Father. Help me to be of help to Scott. I place him in Your hands, knowing you care for him with a deeper love than I do (if that can be!). Put Your arms of love around this child of yours and help him be a blessing and inspiration to all those around him. Amen.

* * *

Friday, September 29 – I lift Scott up to You, and I ask You to watch over him like a mother hen watches over her chicks and a shepherd watches over his sheep. Teach Scott that He who dwells in the secret place of the most high shall abide under the shadow of the Almighty. You are his Fortress. May he learn to trust You implicitly (me too!). Amen.

Saturday, September 30 – O Father, thank You for making it possible for Scott to go on this Walk. Let this be a wonderful time for him....a great spiritual growing experience, and a time for him to grow in his walk with You. Help him to handle each experience by leaning on Your angels all around him. Lord, I feel it is so important for Scott to make a good impression on everyone for Your glory, and also to make everyone more compassionate with retarded people. Thank you, Lord, for what You are going to do. Amen.

* * *

Sunday, October 1 – Dear Father, thank you for this new day. Oh, how wonderful to know that today my Scott is coming home.

Sunday evening, October 1 – Praise You, Father. How wonderful – all the things that happened! ....all the good things they said about Scott. Scott even singing 'He Touched Me' for all the men last evening. The one man told that he 'saw Jesus' while Scott was singing. Thank You, Father. Every prayer was answered abundantly and above all I could think or imagine. You are so good, Lord, so good!

Scott made some wonderful Christian friends during this time. He calls them his 'brothers in Christ.' I'm so glad he had this opportunity to bless and be blessed.

SERENDIPITIES

(UNEXPECTED SURPRISES)

Chapter 16

"The Lord directs the steps of the Godly. He delights in every detail of their lives"

Psalm 37:23 NLT

(*I've seen Scott, time and time again, draw the rest of us closer to one another and to the Lord.*)

One time Lloyd and I were having a disagreement. I don't recall what the argument was over, probably something insignificant, as they often are! Scott, very young at the time, ran up to us and said, "I don't like down talk. I like faith talk!" We immediately stopped arguing. (*"O Lord,"* I prayed that evening, *"keep us talking faith talk."*).

* * *

Scott would not think of eating without saying the blessing. Our whole family knows that no matter where you are, at home or in the fanciest restaurant, we don't eat until we say grace. Barbara and I recall one time we went to a crowded fast food restaurant; and Scott said the blessing, and he went on and on. Finally, I gently kicked him under the table and he ended his prayer. We decided everyone in the restaurant probably thought we were some sort of religious fanatics. I believe even the Lord was amused at the situation.

I explained to Scott that, when praying out in public, you would not want to pray too long, and he has obeyed ever since.

* * *

Scott came home from school one day and said, "We really had an exciting day today!" "What happened?" I asked. "Oh, it was really great!" he replied. "Brian (*a Down's friend*) learned to tie his shoes!" (*Lord, I pray, help us to be this excited about other's accomplishments.*)

* * *

Scott's prayers are so simple, yet so profound. When his dear Auntie, in her 90's, was nearing death, Scott prayed, "Lord, I don't know how to pray for Auntie-O, so I just lift her up to you. Amen." Lloyd responded, "Right on, son!"

* * *

(Serendipity for Valentine's Day, 2000 – On February 14th, Scott read to his Dad and me from his Daily bread (his own personal daily devotional), about saying "I love you" daily to those you love. Scott wanted us to start doing that each night before bedtime. Now, saying "I love you" came easy for Scott and me, but it was hard for his Dad to voice out loud, even though we knew how much he really loved us. Starting that night, though, we each said to the others "I love you" prior to bed.

How precious those "I love you's" are to both Scott and me now – for on February 22nd, a week after we started this habit, Lloyd slumped over at the supper table and was gone to be with our Lord.

* * *

Scott always enjoyed time alone in his room with music. He would play records on his stereo and sing along loudly, using a pencil for a microphone. Someone in the family gave him a real microphone for Christmas one year, but after a few weeks, he was back to using his pencil. It just "felt right" he said. (*Scott still has two favorite pencils that he keeps close by him in the house. His 'security blanket', I presume.*)

* * *

Recognizing Scott's musical interest and talent, I began to pray, in earnest, that the Lord would provide a way for Scott to have an organ of his own. This would definitely take a miracle, for our funds were so limited.

At that time, I had started journaling and writing out my prayers. From my journal on October 23, 1980: *Lord, bless Scott's love of music. Help me to help him in this Lord. Bless our efforts to get him an organ. I see this as something he could do. Maybe it's extravagant, Lord, but I feel it would be such a blessing to him. It will take a miracle, Lord. Help us. Amen.*

In June 1981, the Lord provided. We received an unexpected refund from the gas company, several dear friends (knowing of Scott's desire for an organ) gave him money, and our local music store allowed us to purchase a Lowry-Genie organ with this down payment and a series of monthly payments. The $1200 was, at the time, an insurmountable cost; but now, twenty-five years later, when Scott plays daily on this same organ, I am assured this was a God-incident in his life.

(Serendipity for June 8, 2000 – There was a road surveyor in our front yard close to the deck. I opened the front door and said to him, "You're not going to put the road that close to my house, are you?" He laughed and said they were surveying to make sure that the water did not run back onto our property. Then he said, "I'm really enjoying your music!" I told him that was my 36-year old Down's son playing his organ and that God had given him this special talent. He said, "It's really beautiful! I heard it the other day and enjoyed it so."

(O Father, thank you for Scott and his talent!)

When I told Scott what the man had said, he responded, "You never know who you will touch. It's like that song, Mom, 'Let the lower lights be burning, send a gleam across the waves. Some poor fainting, struggling seaman, you may rescue, you may save.' (song by Phillip Bliss – 1871)

* * *

When Scott was sixteen, he and the other children from his school were 'mainstreamed' into the public school so they would have access to the facilities that other children enjoyed. They were still in their own classroom and had special education teachers and aides that gave them individualized attention. I support this type of mainstreaming, but I do not feel it is fair to 'normal' or 'retarded' children to be put in the same classroom, (and it is *definitely* not fair to the teachers). The special child, of course, needs more one-on-one time and has to learn at his or her own pace.....and the children who can move along at a smooth, steady pace, need to be encouraged to do so.

The year after receiving his organ, Scott played 'Because He Lives' on his organ at his graduation ceremony from school. He was eighteen years old.

(I just have to share with you that Scott was graduating from our Corydon Junior High School. He had attended there two years, and all the kids were offered the opportunity to attend Scott's special graduation ceremony. All of them attended, and they really cheered for Scott, over and over again. It was a special, special day for Scott and our entire family and friends, who came to help celebrate. Our minister was to speak, and a teacher asked me to tell him not to speak about God during the service. Rev. Lyle was highly indignant at this, and said it would be impossible to speak about Scott and not mention God! So he did!)

* * *

A Wise Man - a Scott Story

Our family friend, Jane, asked Scott if he knew what 'cloning' was. Scott said, "It's interfering with God's creation."

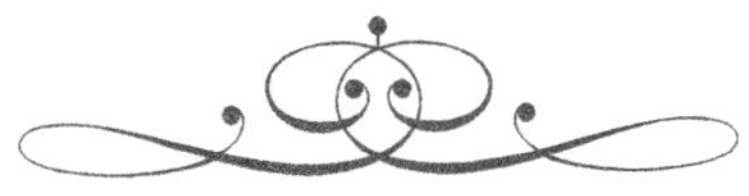

GOD'S NIGHTCRAWLER

Chapter 17

For He will command His angels concerning you to guard you in all His ways....

Psalm 91:11 NIV

Scott was always included in our church youth group; and he participated in a number of summer trips on God's Nightcrawler, a sleep-on bus made for long distance travel. Our pastor, Rev. Lyle, used an incident from their trip out West as an illustration of faith.

Scott has always been afraid of heights but, wanting to join in with the others, he had climbed the 267 steps to the top of Royal Gorge. As they started to descent, Scott told Rev. Lyle that he was very afraid. Rev. Lyle said, "I'll go down in front of you, Scott. You put one hand on my shoulder and one hand on the rail. If you need to stop, you tell me, and we'll stop." Two times on the way down, Scott asked to stop, and Rev. Lyle could hear him pray, "Help me, Jesus." Finally, they reached the bottom, and Rev. Lyle was ready to hurry to join the others. But, Scott asked to stop again, and Rev. Lyle heard him say, "Thank you, Jesus!"

(*Scott taught us all a lesson that day. How many of us pray for things, receive them, and then never stop to say 'thank you'?*)

Philippians 4:6&7 says, 'Do not be anxious about anything, but in everything, by prayer and petition, with thanksgiving, present your requests to God. And the peace of God, which transcends all understanding, will guard your hearts and minds in Christ Jesus.' NIV

* * *

In 1981, Scott again traveled with the youth group on God's Nightcrawler. That trip included riding inner tubes down Apple River (*unbeknownst to me at the time, thank the good Lord!*).

This is my prayer, recorded in my journal, on that beautiful, sunny day - August 16, 1981. *Lord, bless the Nightcrawler.....the drivers, leaders, all the kids at Apple River today. Oh, that my Scott will enjoy himself and be at his best. Lord, heal his breaking out. Help him to take care of his body. Help him to be a blessing to all on the trip. Let him shine out for You. Holy Spirit, fill him. You know all my little anxieties about him, Lord. I surrender my precious one to You. Help me not to worry, but be thankful and trust. Amen.*

When Scott returned from their trip, he told me of his experience on that day at Apple River. They had parked their bus in the huge parking lot, rented an inner tube for each youth and adult, and started down the river. Scott said it was fun for a while; but later, the others all drifted ahead of him a little bit, and he got bored and decided to return to where they had left the bus. So, he waded to the shore, picked up his inner tube, and started walking through the woods to the bus. The only trouble was..... the woods went on and on, and he soon realized he was lost.

Finally, he came to a campsite where he walked up to a man and woman and told them that he was lost. They questioned him, and when he said he came on a "big bus", they loaded Scott and his inner tube into the back of their pickup truck and took him to the main parking lot. There he was reunited with his group. (*Now, I can assure you, if I had know all this was going on, I probably would have passed out! I'm convinced that couple were angels God placed there just to rescue our Scott!*)

* * *

Scott is Touched by an Angel A Scott story by Barb

The youth of Old Capitol recently held a celebrity auction. One item they had on display really caught Scott's attention. It was an actual script from an episode of 'Touched by an Angel,' signed by the shows actors (*yes, even Scott's favorite, Roma*). The script, in

fact, caught the eye of several bidders and was a hotly contested item. The top bidder was Bill Taylor.

Tonight, Scott went to a committee meeting with Joy, Bill's wife. As soon as he got home, he called me and said, "Sister, I've been touched by an angel!" "Is his name Bill Taylor?" I responded. "How did you know?" Scott asked. "Oh, just a lucky guess," I replied. Scott said, "I told Joy to tell Bill to be looking out for me in church Sunday. I'm going to give him a whopping hug! I know that might embarrass some, but I am really touched!"

Bill also wrote a note to Roma Downing, telling her about her special fan, Scott; and she sent Scott an autographed photo with this note, 'Dear Scott, May your life be always touched by an angel. Love, Roma Downing.'

Thank you, God, for placing Bill Taylor's and Roma Downing's in Scott's life!

* * *

...and remember my prayer that Scott would be a blessing to those on the bus trip? Well, God did, indeed, use him I think. The bus driver and his wife thanked <u>me</u> for sharing Scott with them, and told me what a joy it was to have Scott along.

Michael, our grandson, who was also on the trip, said that at share time their last night out, the bus driver's daughter told that Scott was all the time telling her how beautiful she was; and she cried and said Scott was the one who was beautiful on the inside. John West, another boy on the trip, told his mother that Scott sang, 'He Touched Me,' word for word in a deep, booming voice that "sounded like an opera singer." The youth leader, Mary Jean, told me she wished she had the sweet, simple faith that Scott has. *Me too! Me too!*

JUST BEING SCOTT

Chapter 18

"Show me your ways, O Lord, teach me your paths; guide me in your truth and teach me, for you are God my Savior, and my hope is in you all day long."

Psalm 25:4&5 NIV

Scott has always been a blessing to our family. I think God sent him, just the way he is, for a special purpose. Over and over, he has refocused us on love and true values.

* * *

One day, Scott came out of his room, where he had been reading his Bible; and he handed me a piece of paper saying, matter of factly, "Would you please tape this on our TV?" This is what he had painstakingly printed: ***'Turn away my eyes from looking at worthless things. Psalm 119:37.'*** I taped it on the TV and there it has stayed. We've changed TV's several times over the years, but always kept the Scripture. People coming into our home see it, and, I know, it has made us more 'choosey' about what we watch.

* * *

Scott is very patriotic. Abraham Lincoln is his 'all-time favorite' hero. He always insists on reading the Gettysburg Address and a poem Lincoln wrote about his Indiana home on Lincoln's birthday. I often told Lloyd we were probably one of the few families in the U.S.A. who observe the day so faithfully.

* * *

Scott's first brush with death came when his favorite bus driver was killed in an automobile accident. Lloyd and I agonized over how to tell Scott because we had no idea how he would react. We picked Scott up from school that day and I told him, saying, "Scott, Mr. Ripperdan was killed in a car accident today." For a few minutes there was no sound from Scott, who was in the back seat of the car. After a few moments, he began to sing, 'I'll Meet All My Friends in Hallelujah Square,' and he sang all the way home.

Years later, when his most precious Dad died, Scott again found comfort in song as we were driven from the hospital emergency room to our daughters' home.

* * *

Our precious Aunt Mayme was a very vital part of our family. She had been a widow for quite a long time, and we were privileged to have her in our home for a week or two several times. Scott and she were very, very close.

When she died, Scott was standing up by the casket looking at her. I walked up to console him. Before I could say anything, Scott said, "I was just thinking, Mom. You know, Aunt Mayme's going to get to spend Christmas with Uncle Ted. I'll bet they're just huggin' and kissin'!" (*O Father, thank you for this wonderful boy and his strong faith. And thank you for your promise of the hereafter and everlasting life together. Amen.*)

* * *

The Cemetery Critique
A Scott Story

Scott is the only member of our family who truly enjoys visits to the cemetery. One day, we were driving through the cemetery grounds....all was quiet and solemn. Out of the stillness, Scott said, "Numerous dead bodies."

* * *

One December evening as Christmas was approaching, Scott was playing Christmas carols on his organ while Lloyd and I sat quietly listening. It was so peaceful.....lights twinkling on the tree - fireplace burning brightly - soft, carol music floating about us. Suddenly, Scott started playing the 'Happy Birthday' song and sang 'Happy Birthday to Jesus.' Lloyd and I were both overcome with emotion.

* * *

The Women Are in For a Treat Tonight
A Scott story by Barb

Last night, I had asked Scott to go with me to the church women's monthly meeting. I was presenting the program and wanted Scott to sing 'He Touched Me' (which he does a beautiful, booming-voice rendition of). As we got in the car and started off to the meeting, Scott said, "Well, the women are in for a treat tonight!" ....only from Scott!

SCOTT UNLEASHED

Chapter 19

"But I trust in you, O Lord;
I say, "You are my God",
My times are in your hands.

Psalm 31:14&15 NIV

During prayer time in church one Sunday morning, I looked at Scott; he had his Bible hugged tightly against his chest, his eyes shut, and tears streaming down his cheeks. As a mother who tends to be overprotective in not wanting him to call attention to himself, I scringed and hoped no one saw him. When we got home, our seventeen year-old granddaughter commented that the prayer time in church was a special time. She said she looked at my eighty-year-old friend, sitting in front of us, and there were tears streaming down her cheeks, and then she said, "I looked at Scott, and I almost lost it!"

My prayer that day – "Teach me, Lord, to let go and be as uninhibited as my Scott!"

* * *

Many years ago, Lloyd, Scott, and I started having devotions nightly before bedtime. We kept this up every night, including the night before Lloyd went home to be with Jesus.

Scott and I continue to this day. Scott always chooses our theme from his devotional readings, and he picks three songs to go with that theme each night. It amazes me how his choices fit together so well with the theme. I truly believe they are God-inspired, just as a minister can be led in preparing a sermon.

Scott reads his Bible every day and truly knows what he has read. *This year, 2007, is his 18th year reading the Bible aloud straight through.* Time and again, he astounds us with his Bible knowledge. One night in our nightly devotions, I was reading aloud from the second chapter of Acts and, as it was getting sort of lengthy, I stopped before I finished the chapter. Scott immediately exclaimed, "Mom, that's not all of that chapter. You left off about the believers!" (*Sure enough, there it was about the believers!*)

Another time, I was preparing a talk to present to a Women's Emmaus group, and was trying to locate the verse in the Bible that says Heaven and earth may pass away, but God's word will not. I was searching in Psalms, and I asked Scott if he knew where it was located. "Well, I don't believe it's in Psalms," he said, "I believe it's in Matthew where Jesus was talking to the disciples about the end of the age." He picked up his Bible and soon said, "Here it is, Mom. It's Matthew 24:35." (*My heart sang and I praised the Lord. Another of God's miracles!*)

God promises to do more than all we ask or can imagine!
He is truly an awesome God!

* * *

Scott's platform for 2000
A Scott story by Barb

While traveling one day, we were touching on Aunt Mable's favorite topic - 'politics.' Someone suggested Scott should run for president. "Yeah!" Scott said. "So, Scott," I said, "tell us your platform." Without hesitation Scott responded, while emphasizing each point by thrusting his index finger in the air:

"........prayer in school"

"........Ten Commandments returned to schools"

"........no abortions!"

"........and three to four stalls in every bathroom!"

(*You see, when we travel, public restrooms are one of Scott's biggest bug-a-boos.*)

During a trip to North Carolina, we visited a restaurant called 'Gypsy's Shiny Diner.' The waitress came up to our table and her first comment was to Scott. "Hey, haven't I seen you on TV?" (*She probably was thinking of the Life Goes On star popular at the time.)* Boy, that won Scott's heart….he was transformed into a movie star on the spot! (*When we read this paragraph to Scott in 2006, he said, "But I can't remember what I had on my hamburger that day!" Scott holds on to food memories like other people remember specific events.*)

* * *

Since 1999, our family has had our own family web site where we post pictures and stories to keep us connected despite the long distances that keep us apart. I'm still very limited in my computer savvy, but I have definitely enjoyed this aspect of new technology.

Scott stories are often posted on our web site. I'd like to share a few of them with you.

The King and I
A Scott story by Michael

As a visit from Scott approaches, I thought it would be appropriate to relate a story from a previous visit. Before I start, let me point out a couple of things about Scott for those of you who don't know him so well. First of all, he LOVES food. And second, he often preludes a possible offensive statement with some remark such as, "This isn't me talking.." or "I'm not saying I'm mad (hungry, upset, etc) but…." Okay, on with the story.

This took place a few years ago when we lived in North Carolina. Scott, Gram, Mom, Kimberly, and I made the 40 minute drive out to Duncan and Melodee's house for dinner and a visit. On the way out, we decided that we would get some doughnuts on the way back home for breakfast the next morning.

During dinner at Mel's, Scott was already making plans for dessert. Not just that he was going to have it (*Judy's cake*), but that he would have two pieces of it. We kept telling him that he shouldn't even think about dessert until he had finished dinner, but he ignored us. He was staking his claim on those two pieces of cake.

After Scott finished dinner (*about 20 minutes after everyone else finished!*), Gram announced that Scott could have ONE piece of cake for dessert. Scott screwed his face up in indignation, but he woefully accepted and ate his one piece of cake. However, it turned out that Vicki didn't eat her piece and guess whose hands (*and mouth!*) it ended up in? Yes. Scott's! What a grin he had on his face.

Well, this really got me going. Giving Scott a good ribbing is what the Radmacher boys do best, and I was letting him have it, especially in the car on the way home. I told him that I didn't think he should get any doughnuts the next morning because of how much he had eaten that night. But, that got Scott so worked up that he wouldn't stop talking about doughnuts.

So then I said, "Okay, Scott. Here's the deal. You can have doughnuts tomorrow unless I hear you say the word doughnut one more time tonight. And if you do, just forget it. No doughnuts for you!"

Complete silence from the back seat…

But then in a mumbled voice, but loud enough so that all could hear, Scott said, "What I want to say is – Who died and made him king?"

* * *

Scott wanting to say 'you can't have your cake and eat it too' said, "You can't have two cakes and eat them both."

* * *

To say Scott is 'sot-in-his-ways' is putting it mildly! His days and nights are set in stone (at least in his mind), and I often struggle mightily to get him to adapt to the changes that our day-to-day activities necessitate. Our family jokes about it, but I'm sure it frustrates the be-dickens out of them many times.

I've found, through the years, it is much better to give him choices as much as possible instead of saying "now this is the way it is going to be." Maybe that's coddling him, and I know many, even in my own family, feel I coddle him too much; but, after living with him this long, I think I have him pretty well pegged. He definitely has a stubborn streak, and I've seen other Down's children's parents try to deal with this stubbornness by 'laying down the law' and it does not work. So as long as I'm here with him, I will just continue with the methods I've found work best.

* * *

The Bedtime Routine
A Scott story by Michael

This is an account of Scott's nightly ritual...........

At 11:30pm, after the local news and family devotions, Scott begins his journey to sleep. Here's a list, in sequential order, of the things he does before hitting the hay.

1. **Drinks a glass of water.**
2. **Walks around his room and flips the five Scripture verse calendars, located throughout, to the next day. He reads aloud each of the verses. (He says he reads 'kinda fast' to conserve time.)**
3. **Calls Matilda (Scott's pet name for the automated time and temperature recording). He then has his parents guess the correct temperature. (No prizes are awarded to my knowledge.) Finally, he checks the thermometer outside and calculates the difference in temperature between Matilda's and his house.**
4. **Gets his 'bed stuff' ready. What is Scott's bed stuff? Glad you asked. First and foremost is his Bible, which goes under his pillow. Yes, he sleeps with it under his pillow. (A minor emergency occurred on Scott's recent trip to visit us when he left his Bible under the hotel room pillow on the way here... Yes! It was retrieved on their return trip.) Next is a flashlight – also under the pillow.... And a flyswatter! You heard right....under**

the pillow. The flyswatter is for 'shooing millers and moths' that might get into his room. Okay, that's it for under the pillow. Next comes the pill bottles.... One pill bottle contains a roll of Rolaids. The other contains Hall's cough drops. At least when he has a sore throat or cough...otherwise, it's empty. The pill bottles go in his pajama breast pocket or on his nightstand. And finally....he keeps a tube of Chapstick handy.

5. **Next comes the bathroom. I won't go into all the details of this, but I want to hit a couple of highlights. First, Scott informed us that this is where he does his praying. He also has an interesting ritual when washing his face. He rinses his face with water the number of times that is equal to the month of the year (so in November, he is rinsing his face 11 times). He says in January and February he might throw in one or two extra "for good measure."**
6. **Kisses his mom goodnight and gets in bed...around 12:30pm.**

* * *

When we read this list to Scott, Gram, and Granddad, these were their responses. Regarding #1, Granddad says, "that would be a brim full glass of water." And Scott says, "I also put Blue Star Ointment behind my ears and on top of my head and on each side of my nose and on the callus on each foot. Also, Vick's Salve on the tip of my nose."

And, Scott says, "I sleep like a log!"

* * *

(Look in Appendix 2 of this book for more Scott stories.)

* * *

At breakfast one morning, Scott said, "Mom, I'm sure glad the last part of your book is going to be about me. I sure want to read it!" I said, "Oh, Scott, I don't know if I want you to read it or not, you might get stuck on yourself!" "Oh, Mom," he responded, "I wouldn't do that! That's what happened to Solomon, and he ended up dead!"

* * *

Yes, God sent us a special blessing when he sent Scott.

A wonderful poem by Edna Massimilla says it so well. 'Heaven's Very Special Child' speaks of God's careful choosing of a family to care for this special child down here on earth. It says we will recognize it as a privilege to care for this gift from Heaven….this very special child…and that is, indeed, how our family feels about 'our Scott.'

MY STAMP OUT ABORTION SOAPBOX

Chapter 20

My frame was not hidden from you when I was made in the secret place. When I was woven together in the depths of the earth, your eyes saw my unformed body. All the days ordained for me were written in your book before one of them came to be.

Psalm 139:15&16 NIV

For years I nurtured our children and kept our home. Never did I claim to be a good housekeeper, but after I became a Christian, I think I was a good 'home-maker.' After the children were grown and Lloyd retired, I went to work part-time – first, in our local library and, then, in a Christian bookstore, The Faith Hope and Love Shop. How I loved it! My love for books and people meshed to make my work days pure joy for me.

I had many opportunities to witness and share with others…. and; of course, I often shared 'Scotty stories.'

* * *

One incident I will never forget……

A lady was hunting a book for her married daughter who was pregnant. The daughter's doctor had just told her the baby was Down's Syndrome and advised her to have an abortion. She didn't know what to do.

Well, my tongue immediately went into action, and I told her about Scott. I told her what a blessing he is to our family, and how the Lord has used him to bless the people in our church and others he meets. I showed her pictures of Scott when he was on a bus trip to Washington, D.C., told her how he reads his Bible through once a year, how he is a prayer warrior for others, and how he loves the Lord and others completely. She left without a book, but said she would tell her daughter about Scott.

Two years later, a lady came in the store and said to me, "You don't remember me, do you? I'm the lady who told you about my daughter who had been advised to have an abortion because the baby she was carrying was Down's. I went home and told her about your son, and she decided to have her baby. Here's a picture of him." She handed me a picture; there was a beautiful little blond boy, and guess what?....He was perfectly 'normal.' The doctor was mistaken about him being retarded!

My family and friends know how I get 'wound-up' about abortion. It grieves my heart so, knowing that so many children are denied life because they are judged, by some, to be 'unworthy.'

(*If you have any doubt of that, let me tell you that I recently read in the newspaper that pre-natal testing for all moms-to-be, to screen for Down's Syndrome, is recommended by the American College of Obstetricians and Gynecologists. Dr. James Goldberg, who helped develop the guidelines, said a woman might choose amniocentesis (with its' risks) instead of a blood test because "for some couples, losing a normal pregnancy secondary to the procedure is not as problematic as the birth of a Down Syndrome child, so they're willing to take that risk.")* (from the Louisville Courier Journal, February 1, 2007).

The idea that abortion and/or institutionalization are looked on by some people as a solution to the "problem" of Down's Syndrome children really bugs me. A Down's child in an institution would be nothing but a vegetable; it takes people, and motivation, and love all around them to make them bloom. I've been around many, many Down's and other children with wide-ranging disabilities, and I find them all 'worthy.'

Granted, they can be challenging. Even my 'adorable Scott' has a stubborn streak and a slowness of pace that can exasperate even me, time and time again.....and his Dad and I often pondered choices we made on his behalf....and I still have concerns about his future. But the blessings he gives far outweigh any of these concerns.

God is faithful, and I trust him to lead and direct Scott's life today and forever.

ANSWERED PRAYERS

Be joyful always, pray continually; give thanks in all circumstances for this is God's will for you in Christ Jesus.

1 Thessalonians 5:16-18 NIV

When I reflect back over my life (*as, I think, we all tend to do more and more as we grow older*), I see so many times God has directed our paths and answered our prayers. Oh yes, there are some prayers I've received distinct 'no's to, or 'wait' (*which is often the hardest for me!*); and then, there have been those times that I've prayed and prayed over an issue, and it is still unresolved with no clues as to what God has in mind. Those are the times it helps me to read my journals, see how faithful God has been to us in the past, and continue to trust Him.

FRANK'S HEALING

Chapter 21

"For I know the plans I have for you," declares the Lord. "Plans to prosper you and not to harm you, plans to give you hope and a future."

Jeremiah 29:11 NIV

In March 1979, our son, Frank, twenty-three at the time, developed a headache so severe he was hospitalized in our local hospital. After several days, with no relief and no diagnosis, he was moved to Floyd Memorial Hospital (*where our daughter, Barbara, spent her years as a nurse*). A spinal tap was done, showing bleeding in his brain, and further studies revealed a bleeding aneurysm. He was moved into the Intensive Care Unit in critical condition.

The doctors told us the safest choice was to wait at least a week to allow Frank's condition to stabilize on medication, and then do an angiogram to define the exact location of the bleeding. Surgery would then be necessary. The doctors, of course, warned us of the many hazards and risks involved.

How we prayed! ...and our church family and many other prayer warriors mobilized in prayer. I remember how Lloyd, Barbara, and I prayed and prayed as the day for the angiogram drew near. We prayed that they would be able to locate the bleeding area, and that it would be in an area easy to get to in surgery (*if there is ever an 'easy' area to get to in the brain!*).

Well, the day arrived and our family gathered in the waiting room to await the results. When the doctor came out, he said, "Well, I don't have an explanation for this, but there was no bleeding site or problem area that can be identified!" I remember the shocked look we all exchanged, for this definitely was not the answer we expected. OH, but we were glad to accept it!

Praise God! Praise God! Truly a miracle!

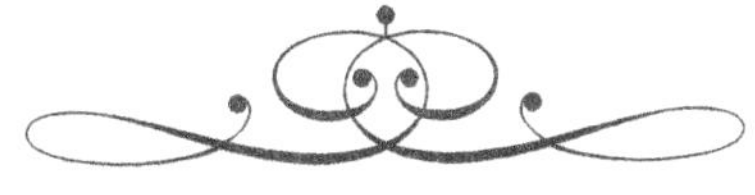

MY OWN PERSONAL HEALING

Chapter 22

"But those who hope in the Lord will renew their strength. They will soar on wings like eagles, they will run and not grow weary, they will walk and not be faint."

Isaiah 40:31 NIV
(my very favorite Scripture)

Three days before Thanksgiving in 1999, I suddenly felt pain-like jolts of electricity in my neck, arms, and legs; and I lost the ability to bear my own weight. For the first time in my life, I was transported to a hospital by ambulance following a 911 call from my dear husband.

There followed days of testing: x-rays, CAT scans, MRI (*all new and frightening to me!*). The results showed bulging discs and much arthritis, so severe that the arthritic spurs were pushing in on my spinal cord and causing the symptoms. (*Now obviously, I would have not understood any of this, but nurse Barbara was there to interpret all of the doctor talk for me.*) The one think I definitely did understand was that I was facing surgery to correct the problems and relieve the pressure on my spinal cord.

Fitted with a huge, very uncomfortable neck brace, I was able to regain some mobility and the pain and tingling began to subside. By the next week when I had an appointment with the surgeon, my symptoms were nearly gone. He said he just wouldn't operate on a woman my age with so few symptoms….(*which was fine with me!!*). He graduated me to a small, soft neck collar that I wear to this day when I sleep to prevent my neck from twisting.

When Barbara and I returned home from the surgeon's office that day and told Lloyd the good news, he 'choked up' and said he had been praying the entire time we were gone that I wouldn't have to have an operation.

The true miracle to me is that, since that time, I've walked many, many miles…visiting Jason and Laura in New York City, walking through the cobbled streets of Williamsburg, and walking and walking and walking on our fifteen-member family trip to Disney World.

* * *

Now, I don't think God intends for us to be Pollyanna's and dole out cheerfulness in the face of crisis; that can turn others off. However, I do think He wants us to turn our thoughts to Him in every situation and trust Him to take care of us.

The Scriptures do tell us not to worry and, though I pray fervently, I must confess; I still 'stew and fret' about things. God isn't finished with me yet, and I'm sure He is still working on me to get me to quit picking up my 'worries' after I've brought them to Him!

Cast all your anxiety on Him
because He cares for you.
1 Peter 5:7 NIV

THE RESURRECTION OF THE MALLARD DUCKS

Chapter 23

So God created the great creatures of the sea and every living and moving thing with which the water teems, according to their kinds, and every winged bird according to its kind, and God saw that it was good.

Genesis 1:21 NIV

My granddaughter, Kelley, has an overwhelming love for animals, a trait I think she inherited from her Granddad. When she was just a little tyke, she would help Lloyd prepare his prize banties for the county fair. They would wash and groom those little chickens, spending hours fluffing their feathers with a softly blowing dryer.

When she came to live with Scott and me after her Granddad's passing, I found her love of all things animal most challenging. She just couldn't pass up a stray kitten or a homeless bunny, and she would beg and coddle me into accepting them into our care.

I found I just had to set some limits on her 'exuberousness' or our pet menagerie would have just over-whelmed us. On one occasion, she was just determined to buy four baby mallard ducks to place on our pond. I thought perhaps a written contract would be the best way to handle the care and upbringing of these new family additions.

Here is the contract as signed by Kelley and myself.

Kelley has my permission to buy 4 mallard ducks.

The agreement is

1.) She will care for them and buy their feed.
2.) If Scott is willing he can help care for them occasionally. (when weather is good.)
3.) They must stay on the pond when old enough.
4.) No way are they ever to be brought in my house.(only the one time when you bring them in for us to see them when they are first purchased.)

Signed: A loving grandmother,

Doris Keller Kemp

Kelley J. Kemp

Well, all went well for several days. The ducklings were housed in our small barn, and Kelley was faithfully tending to their needs. One evening, however, she came bursting through the back door crying hysterically, "Oh, they're dead! They're all dead!"

In her hands she carried all four tiny ducklings....all four indeed...dead. "What happened?" I exclaimed, and she recounted that the ducklings had gotten so dirty in the barn, and she proceeded to give them baths; but, no sooner than she placed the ducklings in the cold water, they all collapsed.

My mind whirled and, knowing I had a load of towels drying in the dryer, I quickly turned off the dryer and placed the ducklings inside, atop the hot towels. I prayed aloud, "O God, you have all power. You can bring these ducklings back to life!" ....and, miracle of miracles, all four ducklings revived and lived to spend many days on the pond.

Later on, their natural predator, a hawk, took their lives....but I thank God my Kelley didn't have to think she had killed them.

FIVE DOLLARS ON THE CAT'S BACK

Chapter 24

"This is the confidence we have in approaching God: that if we ask anything according to His will, he hears us."

1 John 5:14 NIV

Yes, I do think God has a sense of humor. After all, He let me find five dollars on the cats' back! Well, actually, my grandson Jason found it. Here's the story.

Lloyd had taken me to the grocery store (*honestly, one of the few times I did any grocery shopping – Lloyd usually did it and I stayed home with the children*). Anyway, on this day, I had done the shopping and when we got home, I could not find the five-dollar bill I had received as change after paying for the groceries. Now money was very tight for us, and I was desperate in my search for that $5. I dumped out my purse, searched through my jacket pockets and all the groceries to no avail.

Finally, I leaned up against the kitchen counter and said, "O God, please help me find that money!" Just then, grandson Jason yelled from the back porch…. "Come look, Gram, what I found on the cats' back!" I went to the door and there was Jason holding up my five dollar bill. "Oh, praise God, praise God!" I exclaimed…. "there is my five dollars." "But Gram, I found it!" Jason responded. I proceeded to explain to him how I had lost the money and asked him how he had found it. He said he was trying to catch one of the cats and took the grocery box to throw over the cat. "The cat ran out from under the box, and there was the five dollars on her back," he said.

Now Jason and I have had a running joke, in later years, as we have different stories as to how I convinced him that I really needed that five dollars.

OUR JOURNEY CONTINUES

For I am convinced that neither death nor life,
Neither angels nor demons,
Neither the present, nor the future,
Nor any powers,
Neither height nor depth,
Nor anything else in all creation,
Will be able to separate us from the love of God
That is in Christ Jesus our Lord.

Romans 8:38&39 NIV

DAVID'S TREE

Chapter 25

"and the Lord God made all kinds of trees grow out of the ground – trees that were pleasing to the eye…."

Genesis 2:9a NIV

Earlier in this book, I promised I would tell you more about David's beautiful maple tree. The tree stood proudly in our front yard and he loved it so; especially enjoying it during his long illness, when he laid in the shade of the tree much of the summer (*our outside air-conditioning Midwestern style!*), and that last fall, when he sat in the hospital bed we had set up for him and watched the birds and the changing leaves.

Many times he spoke of it as "my tree." In the middle of October of 1964, when we took him to the hospital for the last time, even though racked with pain, he looked at the tree which was in its' full autumn glory and said, "Oh, my beautiful, beautiful tree!" When we came home after David's death, the tree was bare and minus its' glory….(*but only for a season, by God's design*).

Some years after his death, we placed a swing in the front yard and I spent many hours there….snipping beans, sewing, reading, watching the children and, later, the grandchildren at play.

There were actually seven trees in the front yard, and I loved every one of them. Trees are, to me, one of God's greatest gifts to us. I love them when snow is piled on their branches, when the spring buds begin to pop out; I love the shade of their heavy summer foliage and the awesome beauty of their autumn colors.

* * *

I think most trees have their own story to tell…. 'Woodman! Woodman! Spare that tree!' has been a favorite poem of mine since my school days.

Woodman, Spare That Tree

Woodman, spare that tree!
Touch not a single bough!
In youth it sheltered me,
And I'll protect it now.
'Twas my forefather's hand
That placed it near his cot:
There, woodman, let it stand,
Thy axe shall harm it not!

That old familiar tree,
Whose glory and renown
Are spread o'er land and sea...
And wouldst thou hew it down?
Woodman, forbear thy stroke!
Cut not it's earthbound ties;
Oh, spare that aged oak,
Now towering to the skies!

When but an idle boy
I sought it's grateful shade;
In all their gushing joy
Here too my sisters played,
My mother kissed me here;
Forgive this foolish tear,
But let that old oak stand!

My heartstrings round thee cling
Close as thy bard, old friend!
Here shall the wild bird sing,
And still thy branches bend.

Old tree! The storm still brave!
And woodman, leave the spot
While I've a hand to save
Thy axe shall harm it not.

George Pope Morris (1802-1864)

On this particular summer morning it was not a woodman who was going to cut down our beautiful tree, but a local REMC work crew. We had seen them coming up the road, and they were not only trimming the tree limbs back from the power lines, they were almost cutting some of them to the ground.

Needless to say, I could not stand the thought of 'David's tree' being cut down or being trimmed away to nothing. Now, you have to understand, I am not usually a very assertive person, but my love for that old tree strengthened me and, with a very authoritative voice, I demanded that they not cut much of our tree. If they would have not listened, I was prepared to tell them the story of our tree, in order to convince them.

Those dear men must have realized how important an issue it was for me. One of the men climbed up in that tree with his power saw and proceeded to trim, asking me… "Mrs. Kemp, is it alright to cut this little limb?" And hence, I supervised the cutting of a few little branches and they decided it was trimmed enough.

The family, children and grandchildren, laughingly recall the time Gram defended the old tree that is so dear to us all.

* * *

Granddaughter Kelley wrote, "One day I went to my grandparents' house. My Grandma said that Vera had said our tree is the most beautiful tree she had ever seen. Vera and Carlton travel around the world, and they see a lot of trees when they travel. It is very nice of Vera to say that."

* * *

Granddaughter Shannon wrote this poem.

Oh, my beautiful tree!
Oh tree, you are so beautiful to me
Oh, beautiful tree, you are special to me
Thanks for everything you've given to me,
You're the most beautiful tree I've ever seen.

* * *

And I tried my own hand at writing a poem.

Our beautiful, beautiful tree!

In our front yard by the side of the road
Stands a tree we love so well
It makes us shade in the summertime
How many good times we've had there
Would be hard for us to tell.

And now it's autumn time
And our tree in full glory stands
Our beautiful, beautiful tree.
Soon it will be wintertime
The tree's limbs will be bare,
Up will go the bird feeder,
The beautiful tree
Still will share its' branches
With the red birds, blue jays, snowbirds,
And the one lone woodpecker.

Thank you, thank you God
For our beautiful maple tree.

Journal notes November 2001:

Our two grown sons, Jerry and Frank, along with a surveyor and a county road employee, sit with me at the dining table. The men have come to map out some changes they are going to make to our county road. They break the news almost immediately. All the trees in my front yard have to go.

Oh my! Oh my! Not my trees! David's beautiful tree.....the beautiful maple tree that has stood in front of our house for over fifty years!

But.....not wanting to stand in the way of progress, I signed the paper, but not before explaining the importance of the tree, and

I cried when I told them. My oldest son said, "I think you see how important this tree is to Mom."

Well, that was almost nine months ago, and we've never heard anymore about the road changes. I've got to see David's beautiful tree leaf out another spring and make shade for another summer. Thank you, Lord!

* * *

Journal notes July 2002:

Well, the time has come for the trees to be taken.

* * *

Journal notes July 8, 2002:

Tonight granddaughter Kelley came home at 11pm and she said, "Let's go gather a few leaves off the trees and press them in a book, just to remember our beautiful trees." It was a cool evening and so pleasant and comfy under our trees.

I'm trying not to cry Lord, for I have so much to be thankful...a wonderful family, my home, you Lord and all your precious promises. But these trees are a vital link between me and our past as a family. It is so good, Lord, that you made our brains so we can remember. Kelley reminisced about so many things; when she was a little girl, climbing the maple tree, and I would yell at her to get down for she might fall and get hurt.....

she remembered the bird feeder....and all the beautiful birds. She reached up into the branches and found a string we had tied there to hang ears of corn for the birds.

Thank you, Lord, for the ability to remember. Every day I will try to follow your leading so the ones who come behind me will remember the good things. Let our memories help them along in their journey through life.

Kelley placed a leaf from each tree on a sheet of paper and wrote under each which tree it came from. I noticed under the maple leaf she simply wrote 'David's tree.' David....an uncle she never met... but one she will always remember.

"Let the fields be jubilant, and everything in them, then all the trees of the forest will sing for joy..."

Psalm 96:12 NIV

Journal notes July 9, 2002:

By 11am all the trees in front of our house are down. They had pushed them over with a bulldozer, one by one. Even at the last, the maple tree was recognized as a special tree. The construction boss was driving the bulldozer, and I heard him yell out to the other workers, "This is a special tree. I'll saw it down because they want to make something out of it." He had me show him just how close to the ground to saw I....*and then it fell.*

Davey, I heard you say again, "Oh, my beautiful tree!" I just had to cry. But never mind, honey, I know in heaven the trees are more beautiful than any we have down here.

* * *

Christmas 2002 – Kelley made a special Christmas gift for each member of our family. Each one of us received a piece of the old maple tree. She had used a wood-burning tool to etch a branch with leaves on each piece of wood. Above the branch, she wrote:

'God's love endures forever'

Psalm 136

At the bottom, she engraved 'Christmas 2002' and 'made from David's tree.'

GOING ON WITHOUT THE MAIN CHARACTER

Chapter 26

Jesus said, "Do not let your hearts be troubled. Trust in God, trust also in me. In my Father's house are many rooms; if it were not so, I would have told you. I am going to prepare a place for you."

John 14:1&2 NIV

And Jesus said, "Peace I leave with you; my peace I give you. I do not give to you as the world gives. Do not let your hearts be troubled and do not be afraid."

John 14:27 NIV

On February 22, 2000, Lloyd, Scott, and I had just sat down for supper when – with no warning – making no sound – Lloyd slumped over unconscious. Scott reached to hold his Dad up and prevent him falling to the floor, and I called 911. Scott held Lloyd (*who still weighed over 200 pounds)* erect until the EMS arrived. (*Later, I asked him if his arms didn't get very tired, and he said, "Oh, I just asked God to give me strength."*)

Heroic efforts were to no avail, and my precious mate joined our Savior in Heaven. We all said Lloyd went from Scott's arms to God's arms.

Our family and friends gathered together as we prepared for the funeral service.

Oh, how could we go on without our main man?
How could I go on with decisions for Scott....with the house and the chores....with managing our money?
How could I go on without those big arms to hold me?
How? How?

- One day at a time, Doris. One day at a time. –

My God gave me strength, often through the hands of others. Our daughter, Barbara, and her dear husband, Bill, assumed a caretaker role in those first days and nights....their home became our home.

Our sons, Jerry and Frank, were my right hands (*and, at times, my right brain*) in the decisions that had to be made.

Scott, though deeply crushed by loss, was stoic in his responses. He and Lloyd were near constant companions, especially close since the days that I started working outside the home and he and Scott spent their days together. (*Scott says he and his Dad were 'best pals.' He says, "Dad always called me his 'right hand man' and his 'sparing partner'."*) Lloyd would sit for hours and listen to Scott play his organ; sometimes singing or humming along, sometimes keeping time with his foot. Again, Scott's music and singing helped him deal with tragedy.

The days immediately following Lloyd's death are almost a blur to me. However, I well recall the love and support poured onto us by our family and friends. The kind remembrances of others will always stick in my mind.

.........Joey Rosbottom recalled Lloyd always tapping his foot to the music during church.

.........Charlie Lynch fondly remembered his and Lloyd's coon-hunting nights.

.........Carl Snyder said he remembered the night Lloyd bowled a perfect 300 at the lane in Corydon. (*Poor Lloyd. I remember when he came home that night and told me what he had bowled, I said, "Is that good?" How did he put up with me?!*)

.........so many commented on Lloyd being such a gentleman.

..........so many precious memories!

Thank you, thank you, Lord, for the time we had.

Choosing songs for the funeral service was really easy. Barbara suggested 'Precious Memories' (by J.B.F. Wright..1925), and all of us agreed that would be so appropriate. Then we easily chose Lloyd's favorite hymn, 'Victory in Jesus' (by Eugene M. Bartlett...1939).

Three times in my life, I've felt the Lord's presence so close I could nearly reach out and touch Him. One time was when I was looking out our hospital window seeking God's wisdom concerning David's terminal illness. Another time was when our dear boy breathed his last breath here on earth. And then, when we started to sing 'Victory in Jesus,' and we all rose to our feet in that crowded funeral parlor…. (*everyone there to honor Lloyd, but I know Lloyd would have been so pleased that we ended up praising our Lord and Savior, Jesus Christ*).

Yes, the days (*and, especially, the nights*) have not been easy as Scott and I have traveled on without our main man; but God has strengthened us and our days have been joyful. God continues to minister to us with His healing touch through family and friends and through His precious Holy Spirit who resides within us.

Granddaughter Kelley came to live with Scott and me after Lloyd's death and stayed with us a number of years. She married last year, and she and Derrick just had their first baby on July 31st of this year….Logan Scott….my 7th great-grandchild. What blessings!!

* * *

Life goes on. The Lord gives us strength each day!

EPILOGUE

"I want you to trust me in your times of trouble, so I can rescue you and you can give me the glory."

Psalm 50:15 LB

I firmly believe that God works 'everything' for our good… even the bad things that occur in our lives….like cancer, handicaps, deaths or ___________ (*you fill in the blank*). God is able to take every incident and turn it around to make something good come out of it down the road…someday…someway.

GOD IS GOOD….ALL THE TIME.
ALL THE TIME….GOD IS GOOD.

* * *

Know therefore that the Lord God, He is God, the faithful God, which keepeth covenant and mercy with them that love Him and keep His commandments to a thousand generations.

Deuteronomy 7:9 KJV

Following Lloyd's death, we found the above Scripture on a card beside 'his chair,' penned neatly by his own hand. How we treasure the message he left for us!

You see, my friends, God always does what He promises, and He always completes what He starts.

PRAISE THE LORD!

PRAISE THE LORD!

APPENDIX 1

MORE SCOTTY STORIES

Having two goals: wisdom – that is, knowing and doing right – and common sense. Don't let them slip away.

Proverbs 3:21 LB

Palmer – a devoted cat by Barb

Yesterday, Palmer the cat was missing. Scott was concerned but said, "Ol Palmer, he'll be back!" This morning, when Scott went out to feed the animals, Palmer was back. Scott petted Palmer and put his feed in his pan. Then, Scott started to the barn to feed the rabbits. He patted his leg and Palmer followed him. As they walked, Palmer would look back toward his feed (*which I'm sure was enticing him, because he had missed all meals yesterday*), but then, Scott would pat his pant's leg and Palmer would follow. Palmer would look back toward his feed – Scott would pat his leg – Palmer would follow. Mom watched all this from the kitchen window, unbeknownst to Scott or Palmer. Palmer went to the barn with Scott, waited while Scott fed the rest of the animals, then came back to his meal.

Scripture reading – a difficult time by Barb

Mom, Scott and I were making our way home from a visit to North Carolina and Maryland. We decided we would drive straight through.

We had been having a praise song sing-a-long for some miles, when Scott suddenly turned into 'jabber jaws', and we could not get him to be quiet. Mom decided to read us some Scriptures to try to deter Scott's excessive talking.

This dialog occurred:

Mom: "We will now have the reading of the Word, so shut your mouth!"

Scott: "Forgive me for asking this, but how many Scriptures are you going to read?"

Mom: "Just until I get tired."

Scott: "This may be a difficult time."

A Scott quote

"I was astonished, with my eyes wide open!"
(*Scott, our very own Forrest Gump.*)

Scott says: "love soothes anger"

Scott – "plum pacitated"

Scott, explaining why he had done so poorly playing Bible Challenge; "I was plum pacitated!" Frank said, "Do you mean incapacitated?" "Yeah," Scott responded.

The Little Boy in Me by Barb

Last Saturday evening, I took Scott to the 'Light-up Corydon' ceremonies on the Square. It was a beautiful evening, light jacket weather. We stood while the carolers and special groups sang; we walked around the Square and visited with many friends. (The Courier reported that 6000 people participated in the day/evening activities. Gov. and Mrs. O'Bannon flipped the switch to light up Corydon with millions of tiny, white lights.)

We walked through the Square again, enjoying the scene, and, then, we headed for the car. From the loud speaker, we heard the announcement that a very special guest was expected to arrive very soon by horse-drawn sleigh. Scott said, "I know who that will be… Santa Claus!" "You don't want to stay for that, do you, Scott?" I asked. "Well," he responded, "the little boy in me wants to stay to see Santa, but I am a man now…."

……….We stayed.

I Can Hear by Barb

Today, Scott went to his doctor after a head cold and the accumulation of ear wax left him VERY hard-of-hearing. When he got home, he phoned me and, instead of 'hello,' he said, "I can hear! I can hear!" I asked, "Did he get all of that stuff out of your ears?" Scott replied, "Yeah, and it really hurt, but I read in the Bible that women in labor have a lot of pain, but then they rejoice. Now, I'm rejoicing!" (*We all rejoice too, because a Scott that can't hear is a very dull fellow!*)

Mom said that Scott came out of the bathroom the morning of his doctor's appointment and said, "Mom, I can't even hear myself pee!" She said, "Well, Scott, I sure hope the doctor can help fix that, but Scott, don't tell anybody else that." "Oh, I won't," Scott promised. On the way to the doctor, Scott (*not to be denied*), said to our friend Jane, "You know, Jane, there are many things I can't hear. Some of them are personal."

* * *

We were on family vacation at Virginia's Skymont Farmhouse. Michael said, "Okay, Scott, what are we going to do tomorrow? Go on a 20-mile hike?" Scott – "or badminton."

* * *

It snowed and Jerry could not come to get us for our annual New Year's Eve visit in their home. Scott said, "I don't say this, but if I did say it, I would say H-E-L-L." (*Scott was upset!*)

* * *

Scott, wanting to say someone must have Alzheimer's Disease said, "They must have old-timer's disease."

* * *

The Jokester TV Guide by Barb

Scott memorizes his necessary TV shows for the week each Sunday via the TV Guide. According to the Guide, the first show of the new season of Touched By an Angel would be on Saturday September 22nd, so Scott did not go with Mom to an Emmaus Candlelight Service so he wouldn't miss it. It was a re-run!! Scott phoned me and said, "Well, Sis, I think the TV Guide really took me for a fool!"

Menial labor sometimes a pain by Barb

Mom was having Scott help set the table. Scott said, "Put on the ketchup" – "put ice in the glasses" – on and on as he completed each task. Then he said, "Sometimes I wish there was another Scott Kemp!"

Darryl's Restaurant a no-no by Barb

Mom, Scott and I went to a Darryl's Restaurant in Evansville with Michael and Kellar. The room was dimly lit, with lights hanging low over the tables. The waitresses wore short shorts and cut-off tops. Scott sidled over to Mom and said, "Mom, I think this is one of those sin places!" Then he said, "God knows I'm a good boy…" When we got home, he reported to Dad, "I never dreamed I'd get a menu with beer on it!" ……no more Darryl's for Scott!!

A theme for nightly devotions

Scott's chosen theme for the nightly devotions on March 25th, 2004, was 'the Cross.' Scripture reading was Isaiah 53. Scott picked these hymns to sing that night; 'Hallelujah, What a Savior,' 'He has Surely Born our Sorrow,' and 'He Never Said a Mumbling Word.'

We're as good as dead

We were traveling through Tennessee on our return from vacationing with Jason & Laura and Michael & Kimberly in North Carolina. We rounded a bend in the road to see a policeman with his radar gun trained on our vehicle. Scott said, "Oh! Oh! We're as good as dead!"

A 'full day' at the harness races by Barb

Thursday, July 11, 1996 – Today, Dad and Scott went to the harness races at the Harrison County Fair. There were eleven races on the card and, after nine, Dad said to Scott, "Well, Bud, how about we get started home?" Scott looked horrified and said, "What would Mom say?" ….They stayed for the rest of the races.

Scott's three coronaries

Scott: "Well, I have three coronaries!"
Me: "Scott, what are coronaries?"
Scott: "Well, you know. I guess I mean....dilemmas.
Me: "So, Scott, what are your three coronaries?"
Scott: (*counting them out on his fingers*)
"1- my foot" (*a bothersome corn*)
"2- my bowels" (*had to ask to be excused from Sunday School for an 'unscheduled' Bathroom run*)
"3- food" (*forever and always – food!*)

Scott searching for the right word

Scott's prayer for Michael in a stressful work situation:

"Oh, Lord, just really bless Michael in his.... devastation."

Potential greatness by Barb

One day, in the editing of this book, Mom and I were reading aloud the story Rev. Chamberlin had written when Scott was ten; the - I Sure Love That Jesus story. Scott was playing his organ while we read. From the story, we read, 'you all know the youngest son of Lloyd and Doris Kemp. Scotty may never grow up to be the world's greatest philosopher or theologian.' "You never know...." Scott said, from the corner of the room.

APPENDIX 2

HOLY BIBLE TRANSLATIONS

KJV *King James Version*
Wheaton, IL: Tyndale House Publishers, Inc.
Copyright 1981. All rights reserved.

NIV *New International Version*
Grand Rapids, MI: Zondervan
Copyright 1978 – 1984. All rights reserved.

TEV *Today's English Version*
New York: American Bible Society
Copyright 1976 – 1992. All rights reserved.

NLT *New Living Translation*
Carol Stream, IL: Tyndale House Publishers, Inc.
Copyright 1996 – 2004. All rights reserved.

NKJV *New King James Version*
Thomas Nelson Inc.
Copyright 1982. All rights reserved.

LB *Living Bible*
Wheaton, IL: Tyndale House Publishers
Copyright 1971 – 1978. All rights reserved.

AMP *The Amplified Bible*
Grand Rapids, MI: Zondervan
Copyright 1965. All rights reserved.

ASV *American Standard Version*
Public domain.

TNIV *Today's New International Version*
International Bible Society.
Copyright 2001 – 2005. All rights reserved.

CPSIA information can be obtained
at www.ICGtesting.com
Printed in the USA
FSHW010223310320
68646FS

9 781951 886622